Alaskan Wilderness Adventure

*Join Duane and his son Daniel on a
Journey Deep in the Alaskan Wilderness
In Search of Finding a New Home.*

Jath Schmidt

I thank you

Duane Arthur Ose

www.osemountainalaska.com

Duane Arthur Ose

10-2-2013

Edited by rh sterling

Copyright Notice

Contents

*This book is dedicated to my Mother
ADORA MAY OSE (Age 93) who brought
me into this world.
Love you Mom*

Preface

November 17, 1977. I caught a 22 caliber long rifle bullet in the head. The path of the bullet entered through the left lens of the eye glasses. Striking the upper eye lid destroyed the eye. Zipping on, the bullet made its way on back hugging the inner wall of the skull on the left side, between the brain and the skull wall. It plowed an up a trail of bone fragments on its way to the back of the head. Deflecting now went on past behind the Manuela oblongata. (The small brain atop the brain stem) Turning back forward now and stopped in the center right brain. The bullet is in two parts yet today encased in a growth shell protecting from infection and lead poising.

It was deemed inoperable, to be safer left alone then to attempt a removal operation. Needless to say this warrants to be written in more detail in another book. For now I will explain on how these lead me to Homesteading in Alaska and the title of this book. During the emergency operation to save my life and the removal scrambled eye. I had what is known as an out of body experience.

While in this out of body experience, I was tested as to my faith or character. I passed the test or I would have been sent straight to hell of this I am sure. Then a lesson instilled in me. The lesson was: No matter how bad it seems others have it worse. Live by example. Always to do better, not just hoping but to meditate, to reason for the goals intended. I then vowed to enjoy life. This was a destabilizing wound, causing problems to contend with enough to put me out of gainful employment.

Not wanting to live on welfare, the insurance moneys I had coming in would in time end or less en. This would greatly affect my income and life style. About five years went by. At some point my then wife and I divorced and our three children were in joint custody. They were not good times for any of us, not bad but not as good as it could have been. We had our good times, our family times. My father Clarence died one night of a massive heart attack. In the months following his death, I was asked to ride up to Alaska with one of my seconded cousins Mike E. Ose of Wasilla Alaska. The deal was for the summer in Alaska, then Mickey would buy me a plane ticket to fly back to Minnesota come fall.

Mickeys showed me around and on my own of the Alaska country area. My interests were not in the cities or on a road system. I was a country boy at heart. The next year my eldest son, David passed his test for a drivers permit. We then set out to Alaska, a 3500 mile drive from Granite Falls Minnesota 1984. Upon arriving in Wasilla Alaska lived with Mickey helping him build his log home.

It was that summer I learned of Homesteading in Alaska. The two areas open for settlement both of 30,000 acres in size. I became fully armed with all the information, charts, rules, a black and white large photo taken from space of, "The Lake Minchumina Land Settlement Area." I had chosen the more remote of the two areas. Then Dave and I drove back to Granite Falls stopping for a Dairy Queen treat and on home to Wood Lake Minnesota thirteen more miles.

I see my chance to live within my means. To take part of the Homestead Act of 1862 that would come to a close October of 1986 never to reopen again. I had to first visit this this new land. To see for myself then decide whether or not it was meant for me. This could be my last stand in the life. Here I began the story. "Father Son's Alaskan Wilderness Adventure"

Chapter 1 To Be or Not To Be 1984,

While visiting family, in Anchorage and Wasilla I gained many new friends from Homer on North through the farming valley. Hungry for their input, likes, dislikes, from Men, Women, Children, all who were Alaskans. The only complaint came from the Women. They all said it was not the cold winters; they had warm clothing for that. It was from the long winter dark nights of no Sun. For that they had lights, lots of bright lighting and vitamin D tablets. "Alaska is where Women Sleep all winter and keep awake partying during the summer."

During the days of my childhood, I learned to explore on foot my back yard then on outward to experience the land first hand. I was younger then but again this I did here in Alaska. Only here there were mountains, valleys, different plant life and differentness in elevations for weather conditions.

I loved my birth place, the farm, the Minnesota River valley and always will. Not interested in renting or owning a small portion of what I could only afford in Minnesota. I see that here in the last frontier on Earth in Alaska, I could make a new life with the freedoms to breath, to make a new life untethered or restricted of movement. A person can be free in Minnesota as well but I was not ready for a rocking chair for having a gainful employment job was not an option. I could foresee I soon would become bored but here in Alaska I could live again on my fixed income, remotely, live off the land build my own house, trap, hunt and fish.

There was only one more thing to do. That was to find the place or piece of land I would own and live. I looked at State land sale openings but soon there would be many people around me. I could clearly see the future of expansion into the rural areas. It would not be for me in the long term. Not that I do not like people but for my plans I needed room.

Then one day a friend informed me there were two Federal Land openings open for Homesteading. The next day I found my way into the Federal Land Office in Anchorage. BLM "Bureau of Land Management." At the reception desk I told the Women what I was interested in learning more about. I picked up every folder, brochure and a form for filing a Homestead. A staking application or packet they called it.

I then went back to Mickey Ose at "Carefree Acers" outside of the then small town of Wasilla. At that time Wasilla was a small growing town. Mickey was the owner of about 5 acres of wooded undeveloped land in that subdivision. Not much other than a bulldozed driveway, a Small one car garage. The 20 foot Indian Lodge he and I brought up from Minnesota in 1982 and lived in. David my eldest son came up with me this trip age 15 with a drivers permit. We lived in that lodge while David and I built Mickey's log cabin from the trees on his land. (Now the center of his completed house) It was the first experience for Dave and me in building with logs.

Mickey was a skilful pipe fitter making good money on the North oil slope of Alaska. Putting in overtime he sent back each month a large check that I deposited into his bank. Up on the slope there was no need for money, no expenses; it was a working camp the oil company provided transportation to and from work, as well all the needs on the slope. There is more to this to be in another book: But for now between David and me building his cabin. I soaked in the information on the Federal Homestead Act yet open, which was first opened in 1862 to be closed for good October of 1986. There were two land openings, each of 30,000 acres. 1. "The Solana district." It looked nice; it had big trees but was blocked from public access by 11 miles of Native land. Permission would have been needed to access. I was not going to beholding to anyone. Not far enough from people.

It would be just right for some but not for me. Next chance I had went back to the BLM office and bought for $20.00 a high altitude black and white photo of the, 2'nd choice, "Lake Minchumina Land Settlement Area."

The topographic maps as well. Plus of the lands I would need to walk over to get to the land from Lake Minchumina itself. There were lakes to land a plane in this land opening but I wanted to get to know the land by exploring seeing the differences, studying it, to get the full feeling like a sod buster farmer would the land he claimed way back in the early years of 1862 on of homesteading.

64 claims had been filed soon as the Lake Minchimina Area was open, most the same day of the opening December of 1982. All the best shore lines were claimed of the 5 or so tundra ponds or no named lakes. Two shallow to be worth anything or dependable, save for the mosquitoes that loved the low lands. Being of Norwegian decent I loved the hills. A good lake would have been nice but in this settlement area there were no decent lakes.

Permafrost is prevalent in all low lands and areas sheltered from the Sun in this district. (Permafrost runs 1,000 feet deep) Building on stilts was not an option for me. I wanted a high country hill side facing the Sun overlooking the tundra ponds and swamps. No, my plans were not to get off a plane and build something that would not last. Or without a long distant view of the McKinley Mountain Range. Besides it would be cold in the bottom land. Cold sinks, don't yah know?

Mike Houseman from Minnesota made arrangements to fly up and spend a few months with us. Then help drive back down the Alaskan Canadian Highway. Mike is a good friend of mine and lives outside of Willmar Minnesota. With his help David and I closed in Mickey's log cabin before the snow came. Not soon enough for Dave to start his school year in Wood Lake. David had enrolled in the Wasilla high School, till we were ready to drive south the 3,500 miles. We made that trip in a record time of 3 days. Only stopping to eat fuel and stretch our legs. Traveling on this highway in early fall is not wise due to unpredictable weather conditions. So it was a race for more than one reason. Main thing was to get David back in school.

Chapter 2 – Be Prepared

Spring of 1985 Daniel my youngest son and I drove up to Alaska from Minnesota and prepared for the hike, in search of new land. Soon after the school year ended, we loaded our camping supplies. A four man Eureka tent, sleeping bags, mountain internal frame back pack, external frame back pack, tube container for rolled up maps, topographical maps, the black-en-white photo of the settlement area; charts, folding grill, frying pan, cooking oil, light weight camp kittles, camp plates, eating utensils, water proof matches, spices, bars of soap, tooth paste, toothbrushes, towels, wash cloths, toilet paper, extra changes of clothing, leather gloves, hats, box of pic coils (kills mosquitos), rain gear, roll of duct tape, large section of clear poly sheeting, 100 feet of ½ inch rope, (journal), two pens, 35 mm camera, film, Mossberg short barrelled 22 cal. rifle, 500 rounds of 22 cal. long rifle bullets, white metal detector, two three foot gas welders rods of 1/8 inch diameter (for dosing), two pocket knives, two whistles, compass, (no GPSs Available) 4 canteens, Iodized purification tablets to kill the water born germs, (Bad Water can Kill, giardia is a consuming parasite that will leave no food value to you.) one east wing hand ace, machete long knife, hunting knife, Fishing gear, army jungle boots, entrenching tool, head nets, 4 containers of mosquito repellent (best are Bens 100 deet & Musk oil), back packers cord, fanny pack full of first aid to include sutures' for sewing closed open wounds, antiseptic, six red distress signal air burst flares and signal mirror.

Not being prepared or properly educated in the art of survival has killed a young man several miles east of my now homestead. Not for the lack of food but what was in his belly eating the food before he could utilize the food. It is a tiny parasite (Giardia) that multiplies living in your small intestine giving you a slow diarrhea death. Commonly called beaver fever the only cure is to take antibiotics and soon.

We were prepared to live off both the land and what we carried on our backs. While in the Army I was trained to survive. Then later became a Scout Master for the young men of Wood Lake, Minnesota. I grew up with my experiences in exploring the granite rock quarries in the rugged parts of the river valley of Minnesota. (Called the Rocks)

Then while in Wasilla holding up with Mickey Ose, we bought a short barrel Mossberg 12 gauge shot gun with a sling 15 rounds of triple 000 buck, 15 rounds of magnum 3 inch slugs. This was our bear gun. Every other round loaded in the Mossberg short barrelled shot gun would be a slug or 000 buck shot. Enough freeze dried back packers food for two, for a month. The 22 rifle would bring down birds and rabbits for fresh meat. (Rabbit is low on food value)

For a backup plan I bought way more then we could carry on our back. That was canned goods that we would leave behind inside the air strips building at Lake Minchumina. Then more gear and as deemed too heavy later was tied high above the ground of the shore line before we went inland, safe from bear and out of sight. A tree was blazed to mark this cache. In case we for whatever reason would have to fall back. Dan turned age 15 near the end of June that year and I was 43 when we left Wasilla to Fairbanks. Mickey had a good long heart to heart talk with us like the caring person he is. He questions my motive to make this trek into the wilderness that was to be for a long time. As well as making a home in the wilderness. Mickey is a people person as most people are. The difference is some are meant to live with people and others are not or prefer not to be. There are the want to bees, dreamers that jump right in to trouble without any experience. Those are the ones that get themselves and others killed. Someday others may want to fallow my footsteps because of this book, web sites, or other books I plan to write. Be it known what I have done was not done by chance but from the skills, training and experiences I have.

The future is what we make or in my case could see ahead. Technology was coming on fast in the way of communications, travel, we have only to look to the past to see how fast new ideas advance like dominos, and progress will not stop anytime soon. I wanted only to be ahead of it. (Like off topic) [Cancer will be not only curable but preventable in our near future. Also stopping or controlling the ageing process.] I may not live to see this but you the readers might. Morning of July 2 we were on the road. Taking most of the day to drive the 300 miles from Wasilla to Fairbanks on what is called the Parks highway. We had supper late that day. Drove back down the high way out of town to a pull-out parked the pickup and slept. Next morning, after breakfast, we made our way to the international airport of Fairbanks. Tickets for a one way flight to "Lake Minchuminna" were $75 each. There we were weighed along with our gear. Our packs and gear was put in storage to be put on the plane the next day. The big day finally arrived. Parked the pickup in long-term storage where it would be safe.

Chapter 3 - Day 1, July 4, 1985

The young lady at the ticket counter asked us if we were going to the Lake for trophy fishing. Then she went on to tell us that a lot of people go there for the big fish. I then made the mistake of telling her that we were going on a hike to the "Federal Land Settlement Area" to find land to stake. The look on her face was telling me she thought me to be a crazy person. I said no more.

This flying service was a small air taxi service that had scheduled flights two times a week to this lake. Lake Mininchumina is the largest inland lake in Alaska. The lake is only about 25 feet deep but the fishing is great. At one time about 42 people lived on the shores of the Lake, they once had a school, now (2013) less than nine live there. The lakes air field has a weather cam automated station that anyone can pull up on the computer and it used quite regular for pilots. The airstrip itself was made for B-29 bombers during World War 2 at that point we ferried planes by air to Russia.

While we were waiting for the plane to be loaded and ready, Dan had a special request, he wanted a window seat. I said sure Dan. Then it became time to board. The plane was parked on the Tamarac. Dan was looking around. What are you looking for Dan? Is that small plane for us Dad? Sure is Dan. I don't think you will have a problem finding a window seat, they're all window seats. It was a twin engine Chief Cherokee that held six passengers, two pilots and cargo. The residents of the Lake utilize this service for their supplies flight service and mail. At $75 each one way it was very reasonable to travel to town and back, unlike the expense of private charter services.

At the lakes airstrip there was a small shack of a post office. One of the lady residences was the post office mistress. This post office is still operational. Even today, (2013) only about nine people use it two times a week. This post office has been on the chopping block list for some time but somehow has managed to survive. Our Tax Dollars at work. During the flight, one of the passengers, a young lady with her child struck up a conversation with us. She was coming home from a shopping trip in Fairbanks. This woman has made several trips like this. As we travelled she pointed out points of interest. When we became near Lake Minchumina, Bear Paw Mountain came into view. Shortly after that Mt. Roosevelt, then a wide meandering river named the Muddy, which flowed out of the lake.

This was the first time I seen the Lake. This lake was very beautiful. With many smaller lakes, the river with low lands, forest to northwest were the higher hills covered with white spruce and birch. From this vantage point we generally could see the route that Dan and I would take. There were no roads or trails only vast wilderness.

The few people that lived around the lake had a wonderful view of the lake. I can only imagine how rough that water could be in a windstorm boating on this lake could be treacherous for sure you would not want to be caught in a windstorm. Looking down at this lake, there were no boats seen at all, unlike the lakes that you'd see in Minnesota that would be jam-packed with boats and water skiers.

Other than seeing the small cabins, dog yards, airfield with runway lights, a few buildings, it appeared as if we were in another world. We were dropping down to approach the airstrip, there was a across wind on approach wheels were lower and locked the plane straighten up on the runway. It was a smooth touchdown rolled to a stop.

In a moment the engines were turned off and the post office lady was there for her mail exchange. A young man on a four wheeler with a trailer drove up alongside to haul cargo away. We all disembarked, and then people began to approach us. The arrival of this airplane was akin to having a stagecoach arriving with the mail and new people.

I must describe the difference between living in the so called civilized world and arriving in nowhere. In the civilized world there is noise 24-7 here after all engines were turned off; there were only people voices, otherwise a deafening silence. Then the pilot said it's time to go. He said that because the mosquitoes jillions of them were approaching swarming attacking us zzzzz noise was getting louder as they neared us.

In Fairbanks they have mosquito control but here it was every man, women or beast for themself. Fortunately, I anticipated this from experience and had a bottle mosquito repellent in my pocket. Daniel said, gee whiz, thanks Dad. I said wait till we have to use the head nets on a cloudy day when there bad.

Today was Fourth of July the locals had prepared to set off fireworks at midnight the darkest time of the day, for you see were still in the times long daylight.

June 22 thereabouts is the longest day 24 hours the sun. Or I should say 21 hours in this latitude, but is never too dark to read. Thus the late-night hours to have the fireworks display still long sun hours. Along with a rock skipping contest a yearly event held out on a spit of land that extended out from the shore line, flat lake stones are used.

We were quickly greeted and invited to celebrate Fourth of July. This was a tempting offer to get to know everybody, but I had other plans. A couple of men and a woman approached us inquired as to what we were going to do. This was not like being in a big town where we would be ignored. Here we were strangers for only a short time.

Upon learning that we were headed out on a month's journey in the wilderness the woman gasped and looked at Dan. Then told us only 7 other party's tried to do what we were about to try. Then told us none made it and most came back in a day. One was gone for over a week. He went in unprepared and without misquotes repellent. Thought he could live off the land with only a pocket knife.

When he came back to the air strip he had said he contemplated killing himself due to the mosquitos, black flies and all the other blood sucking bugs. He was being drained of blood alive, was lighter and had not eaten. He's flesh was like raw meat, swollen red, bad rash and looked infected. Somewhat like a burn victim.

This news only encouraged me to push on even more. Confident now that my experiences would be proven. After the women left, a native man spoke to us. He casually checked us out for the supply's needed. Then told us it was not the bear to worry about but the "little people". I thought to myself then but did not ask what he meant by that. I was thinking he was only trying to express his beliefs or something. Only thing, he was serious and it was said to us in confidence as he looked over his shoulders.

It was not till June 1987 the summer of, did I then experience up close the "Little People." This too is for another book. With that we went about checking our gear organizing and stowed the extra food and some clothing in a storage building by the small post office that was secured and locked. In the event we would return for whatever reason. My plan was of the 64 already homesteaders out there. There would be a plane that we could catch a ride out to town after I had found or not the land to stake.

Mind you, Staking was an option that had to be thought out well. To be sure of after my boots were on the ground itself. I never buy anything without first inspecting. Like a woman, compatibility and love are the key deciding factors. The land itself would call to me. Are we ready Dan? My mountain internal frame pack with attached gear on my belt weighed close to 100 pounds. Dan's external frame pack with the attached gear was close to 80 pounds. We would be in super low gear moving with this weight. In the case of the turtle that won the race so it was with us.

As planed a year ago on the topographic maps our route was laid out in general to be adjusted as needed. Where's the yellow brick road, Dad? I said the shore line that away.

Getting a late start we did not make it far this day but it was a start to establish our routine. This air strip is on the south west shore and we had to travel westward before we could go inland to the high ground and then north east following the shore and some in the woods was to be our easiest part of the hike. There was a trap line trail for a ways but the lake was used most, summer or winter for traveling by the locals.

Chapter 4 - Day two
July 5, 1985

Morning came sunny and bright with a light breeze off the lake. This breeze and being on the shore kept the mosquitos away. The tent was a four man eureka with a rain fly this made for a breathable tent. Pancakes were for breakfast using our silver tone frying pan and the potable folding grill, this grill was attached to the outside of my pack. Laugh if you must but this hike was not your ordinary hike. It was a one way hike off of the beaten path. In fact there was no path at all. We were traveling most likely where no human has gone before after we leave this lake.

This morning's view was an inspiration. We were camped on the shore of the largest inland lake and about 6 miles from the geographical center of Alaska. We had a clear view of Denali Mountain and its range. Denali Mountain (Mt. McKinley) the highest in North American, 20320'

The shore began to narrow and become rocky. It came to a point where it was no longer possible to follow. Looking further ahead we could see it was clear. At this point the water was too deep to wade; we had no choice but to climb this high hill going over the top on down back to the shore. As we were climbing, a plane with floats landed and came to shore where we had been yesterday. Two people one a pilot guide the other a tourist. I could only imagine the expense this was for the tourist. They went into the woods and to the high ground for a look out view of the lake and the mountains some 60 miles distant. We stayed still till they left to give this tourist his time to feel alone getting his money's worth. They never noticed us, some eighty or so feet away in the thick forest of white and black spruce. Then we moved on. The rest break was needed anyway.

Top this hill and a short distant inland, we come on to a well-used trail It was favorable to the direction we were headed. It lead us to a sizable cabin lived in by a man and women. The man was busy doing dog chores. We introduced ourselves to the woman to ease her mind. They were residents of the community. Most likely they had heard of us. The lady went on to tell us best she could about what we were in for on this journey. Then looking to Daniel straight on asked him what he thought knowing what he had just been told. Dan responded without hesitation, telling her thanks for your concern lady, but we will be fine. This hike has been planned and prepared for over a year. My Dad has years of experience most all his life Mam.

She added that we would be on our own in case of an emergency it will be buggy and the walking will be treacherous, looking at our heavy packs, shot gun, 22rifle, and the metal detector in our hands. I noticed that look, then said whatever we might need are in these packs. You might realize we have planned on a long argues hike. We were told of the seven parties' that turned back they were unprepared and wise to have turned back. We might have to too. In fact we left extra food in the shack by the post office in case. As a Scout Master "Be prepared" is the Scouts motto. I am not some fool that is about to try to survive on only a pocket knife when we had a year to prepare. About the medical emergency's I pointed to my fanny pack this pack has all our medical supply's needed. I assure you I have prepared well. After leaving the couple and their cabin following what must have been a winter trail. We then made our way from the winter trail to the shore line. But in doing so we were getting our first case of the matted jungle mossy floor, brush, snags, stooping under, climbing over, crawling kind of travel. This is was what was in store for us. In some areas, the moss covering the ground was all of 2 feet thick. The moss had many surprises for us hidden from view. Once again we were back on the shore. At times on this shore we had to wade through the water. A test for our jungle combat boots they would get wet but then the water would drain. We were finally done wading in the water our pant legs were wet which was a cooling effect from the breezy winds off the Lake. As a precaution, changed our jeans, the jeans were hung on our packs to dry as we walked.

With heavy packs we moved slow resting every chance we had or coming upon convenient bench rests nature had made. That way we could take a 5 min. in place rest leaving our packs on. Sitting on the ground with a heavy pack was no fun in getting back up. To remove the pack and then put them back on was a two person job difficult for one. Dan spotted the dead fall first with the roots all pulled up. It made a perfect bench. Dan sat on it giving a sigh of relief. Dan carried the nearly 80 pound pack. Dan was smiling from ear to ear, as I just stood there resting in place.

Then his smile left, as we heard a little crack then another. Dan just looked at me as the tree went all the way to the ground with a crunch! Thousands of ants were madly milling about.

It was a funny sight. I had to capture this on the camera. Then he had to be helped up, the full pack held him down like an upside down turtle.

Little ways further we picked out a high sandbar for the days end. We set up the tent, a cooking fire and ate some of our food that was weighing us down. After supper it was still plenty of light so we just relaxed some and took in the sights sitting by the campfire. Looking on into the woods we seen a jungle and wondered how our inland trip was going to be. I told Dan the woods are the worst near the bottom of a hill and then thins out as we go up. The bottoms are wetter making for dense willows alder and a tangle of brush. We are going to stay up on the top and go down only to get to another hill on up again to a ridge top. The route will not be direct but easier to travel saving us time, less risk of falling and away from all that jungle over burden growth.

My hiking experience in Alaska taught me that. The good news is, here north of the range at least in these parts there is no "devils club." That is a nasty shrub with large leaves that hide two or so inch long sharp thorns on the underside of the leaves that are as big as elephant ears that can rip your cloths and flesh to shreds. When hiking in the Matanuska valley by Sutton and Palmer south of the range. That plant is at the base of all the hills and on the brushy low lands.

That Mossberg 12gauge shot gun Dan, has six rounds alternating from triple 000 buck to a single slug all are magnums. Well then, let's see what they can do? See those tall tree stumps over there. The one that's 10 inches in diameter Dan! Stand back 15 feet. Aim and fire at the mid-section pretend that would be a bear. Dan was all for this. Yeah! It was our first time to try this new weapon. "Kerr Boom!" No more tree. Holy cow! Dan said. I blew it away. Now you know what a triple 000 buck does. Try the next round. It is a three-inch single slug magnum on the tree next to the one you just shot. Dan took Aim and fired! Kerr Boom! Wowy Wow! Holy Cow! Dan said. The single slug made a 1 inch hole on this side of the tree and busted up the tree into splinters going out the backside.

The pump action shot gun was loaded full of six rounds, but never a round in the chamber till needed for safety reasons. My policy was never to have a round in the chamber until needed. The shotgun is loaded having every other round a single slug and triple 000 buck. After supper we called it a day. Then we heard the sound of a motor boat. This brought us out of the tent. It was some of the people we had met at the airstrip. Visited us for a bit then offered to come back in the morning and give us ride to a shore line where we would move inland from there. Such an offer would save us two days at least. It was agreed upon they said see you in the morning.

Chapter 5 - Day Three, July 6, 1985

Along the breezy shore we could keep relatively misquote free. We were enjoying breakfast and the coolness of the morning. It's time to break camp Dan. We were ready and waiting for a boat ride. A call came from the lake "Ahoy a shore!" Good morning! Our new friend had a 20 foot flat bottomed long and wide boat. We put our gear in first then climbed in. He then asked where about you'd like to be dropped off at. I pointed to the spot and off we went.

This gentleman was in the process of building a new cabin down the shore a ways then about three hundred feet in the woods. Today he was just beginning to set the sauna tubes for the pilings the foundation. In this area there was permafrost and that was the only correct way of building a structure. The ground under the cabin must remain cool and covered with moss or a cabin like so many other cabins had, would sink as the permafrost thawing slowly inch by inch.

We asked him how much it costs to live here. He replied: About $100 per month. When I need money I hop a flight to Fairbanks and go to the job hall for a cash job or a longer surveying job. He was a surveyor by trade. In about 5 minutes' we reached the shore. Thank you very much sir. He wished us luck turned about headed back out to the lake. This ride saved us a lot of time, energy, supplies and hard effort. Maybe two days because of the boggy inlet side of the lake we would've had gone around crossing it where we could and then on up the hill.

It was here on the shoreline. We hung up on the site items that we could spare to leave behind. I thought of the early homesteaders making there cross country journeys. Having to lighten their loads as well, it was the glass foremost that was hauled along, the windows they held onto were the most cherished, even crazy things like a piano. For us, we left on this shore was the extra changes of cloths, the rest of our canned goods, fishing rods, (keeping only the line and hooks) rain pants, and a few other non-essential items that a week end camper on wheels might bring.

There is some truth to wearing the same clothes a year at a time and washing in the summer or spring. All these things filled an Army duffle bag. There Dan, our packs are now lighter. Then tossed en end of our rope over a limb way up high and pulled the bag up high out of sight for neither man nor bear to see. Blazed a nearby tree like the pirates of old would have marked there treasure. We used 50 feet of our 100 foot of rope doing that. We still had 15 days of back pacers dehydrated food. Salisbury steaks, several other choice meals, all light weight, sealed and safe.

From here on we will have to be very careful and make every step carefully, plus we would be on our own, far from the Lake. To make our way up this forested long sloping hill would take the better part of a day I left Dan behind with the gear, while I went out ahead with red survey tape to mark a trail. It was a gradually sloping hill for a good half-mile rounding to a level, near the top then it became easier. Several hours had past; at that point I turned back to the shore.

It was full of alder trees and a tangle of weeping alder limbs. I had laid out the trail we would take. Going back down the hill with my long machete knife cleared away the limbs. Based on this climb, flagging, brushing, it was not hard to decide what to do. Dan, I decided the best is to make camp here on the shore; we will have a long day's work out tomorrow. (Moose eat surveyors tape in time)

Our goal was to make the journey safely. This meant to go slowly, to think three times before a choice was made. Never carry a gun with a round in the chamber, (Never trust a safety switch) always check the compass. Make no short cuts. Travel through birch forest whenever possible because a spruce forest was obstructing. To fallow the high ground by doing this it would make traveling safer, less moss covered ground, less brush, and to see far for getting our bearings off land marks marking our position on the maps for the way we want to go. The low areas would be a jungle and impede our travel. This was a North America wilderness jungle. Not for a horse and rider but only in other places of Alaska.

My observations of the flight from Fairbanks and now at this lake has been this: On the shore line the rock had been crushed into gravels away from the steeper jutting rock formed hills of jagged broken cubical black basalt rock smoothed by the action of the lakes seasons. There was some shale gravels but mostly cubical basalt with a mix of quartz. What I had seen during the two days, the lake had worn stones. The rest was not disturbed or moved since it was formed.

There was not much soil covering the bed rock except in the pockets and boggy ground. No volcanic ash, silt, or glacier action. There once was a sheet of ice covering this area it had not moved or drifted but slowly melted in place forming lakes, tundra ponds and meandering winding rivers. Only in places was the remaining glacial ice covered by the blown dust storms and shielded from the sun and warming air, keeping the ice frozen in places. In fact yet today the cores of some hills or ravines are of ice and soil covered. It is common to dig into the permafrost soil covering and collect ice formed millions of years ago. Millions of years of extreme penetrating cold, froze the land deep as much as 1,000 feet here in some regions of Alaska and parts of Canada.

I had seen windblown drifted sand dunes on the flats like the snow drifts in the mid-west States after a northwest blizzard, riffles from one direction of the wind during the flight out from Fairbanks, not only windblown sand dunes but puddle-ling. Within twenty to thirty miles of here the puddle-ling was generally absent. The dunes and the puddle-ling ridges had been covered by ground covers of mosses and trees.

There were small tundra ponds, some of which were in the center of a circle of spaced apart at regular intervals, ridges outcrops or fault lines, as though the ground had been shaken or otherwise collapsed. The centers sunk forming ridges, much like in the ripples on a pond after a stone is tossed in the center. There was puddle-ling without tundra ponds too, I refer to these as puddle-ling; something is under those puddle-ling areas. I suspect oil, gas, or both.

Also to see exposed rock from the air was rare only the broken off river hills and river banks was there rock. The rock was covered by windblown materials. Like that in the desert of Arabia. Save here in this area there was green vegetation covering that with wind drifted material. But then what do I know I have no degree; I am only a simple rock hound here on planet Earth. Are you getting the Idea now why I carry a metal detector and the dosing rods?

Chapter 6 - Day 4
July 7, 1986

Having a big breakfast, loaded up, took one last look at the lake, and then began our ascent into the interior. The real test was at hand. It was like climbing out of the trenches onto a battlefield, going forward into the unknown of man's land. This time we placed head nets on over our hats covering down to our shirts tightly. Wore leather gloves after an applying Bens 100 deet on the clothing only, not the skin. This was done before we set off into the forest of darkness. Black flies, horse flies, and mosquitoes, no seeums and every blood sucking bug known to man awaited us except wood ticks.

Our hands had to be covered thus the gloves. It was not because of it being cold, we wore long sleeves covering are bodies. This was July the warmest and hottest time of the year reaching 100 degrees during mid of day. (Interior temps are colder and hotter than the Anchorage areas) Two hours later we reached the summit, this was a long time but considering what we had to go through not bad. Our Vietnam jungle combat boots were already proving themselves, plus the soul inserts in them to keep from getting blisters. Checking with a topographic map set our heading that would be heading generally in the north-easterly direction. The ground was fairly flat with no drainage, black spruce were the prevalent trees, moss covered grounds was 2 feet thick and very treacherous.

Unable to see distances more than 25 to 50 feet at a time. We only had a compass to rely on it. It was a very dark closed in forest. I was reminded of open space by the lack of it here, feeling of claustrophobia was pressing in on me.

This is a common experience throughout the trip, not knowing where we are except following the compass heading, always trying to follow the highest terrain never to go into a ravine or downhill. That often meant meandering and referring to the compass quite often. Our need of consumption of water was quite often, I was quite well aware of dehydration. It is important to hydrate as often as we could.

Having a large 2 quart canteen and two smaller one quart canteens was very crucial to this trip. We will also be on the lookout for water sources. Sights and sounds of flowing running water was always a pleasure to hear. I stated earlier all-important pure drinking water was all the water was purified not by boiling on this hike but by Iodized tablets one pill per quarter water shaken not stirred. Only rainwater for a water source or sources coming right out of the ground was deemed to be safe to drink. Topographic maps are very handy useful in the location of finding water, those suspected water sources were always targeted for our next camp. At times it was morning, before we made camp in order to get to a water source to replenish our canteens for washing and cooking at each camp. When we had stone available we built a fire pit of stone.

Always putting the fire cold out with water was another reason for water. It would be easy to start a forest fire that would ignite days later if the ashes were not cold out. I would not have liked to look back two days later and see a fire raging behind us. This could very well happen due to rotted vegetation on the forest floor. I cannot emphasize enough: that a campfire on rotting roots running through a fire pit is but a fuse to ignite a fire. Wherever possible, we would choose rock for a camp fire at each campsite. If there was rock available. We made a small rock walled camp fire alter is what we called them.

Instead of tearing it down after we were done we let them stand for whatever reason, someone might come across them or if we had to comeback this way the campsites would be our guide, at each of our campsites we would deeply blaze a tree and flag the area with our survey tape, to be seen from a distance. As we travelled every so often a healthy tree was blazed on both sides so they could readily be seen from either direction. The blazing of a tree properly must be blazed to the heart wood exposing widely the heart wood. Not just the outer bark. All these were precautionary measures in case we had to return or someone to find us. Blazing the trail would be a clue that someone would have in searching for us or our remains.

In some of the dark areas of the forest buried under the moss there was still ice. This ice we used in cooking our freeze-dried packages of food saving our precious water for drinking. We travelled one whole day; it took us down between two ridges. At times it became necessary to go down to get up on the next ridge in our course. This was one of those days, I felt less human traveling in the dark dense black spruce forest. The end of the 18 hour day, we had not yet reached a creek or could we see out to get landmarks to locate on the map where we were. All we knew was that we were on the right direction but where was the question. Drinking lots of water was important, not to the point that we would run out, there were times we had to ration to be safe. This was the case two-day.

We cleared an area for the tent, fire pit, no rock but beneath the moss cover was plenty of ice and hard frozen ground. The folding grill with legs would work well. Placing more dry moss where the self-supporting 4 man tent would be for a comfortable sleep.

The tent had a cloth floor but was not water proof so we had cut a clear poly sheet to put down under the tent first. I knew about vapor barriers and sleeping on damp ground. The tent was then set up placed our sleeping bags and packs inside leaving only the cooking tools outside.

Never leave a tent unattended. It has been my experience that any size tent smaller is too small for those serious two people back packers. Besides this one was light weight durable, breathable and bug tight. The Army has two man pup tents that are so small a squirrel can't fight his way out of when needed to move out in a hurry. I know, as an Army aggressor I tagged many a soldier while they were trying to get out of a pup tent.

In order to conserve water only for drinking me then with a pocketknife, a hand axe removed the thick layer of moss and dug ice and frozen earth. Then placed a layer frozen matter in the pan, then the foil package of steak with a covering of ice then cooked till done. (One does what you must do in the bush). Supper was delicious filled the hole. Want me to heat some water up for doing dishes Dan asked? Nope here we use moss, scrub and the moss disinfects at the same time. We need to conserve the water and melting ice would have to come to a rolling boil for 5 min to be germ free. Moss works better.

In the tent now we could remove our head nets and gloves but before removing more there was one more thing to do. What's that Dad? Close the zipper Dan. How many mosquitoes in here I asked? Eight or ten Dad, break me off a ½ inch length of pick from a coil of pic Dan. Because were closed in a whole coil might kill us. 1/2 inch will do. Watch and learn Dan. I held a lit match to the piece of pic; it began to glow and smoke. The mosquitoes were buzzing about as they did they would fly over in through the smoke rising from the pic, when they flew into the smoke they dropped dead instantly with a thud. Neat Dad! Let me finish off the rest. For ever more Dan took care of the mosquitoes in the tent.

We talked of tomorrow's hike of guessing how many miles we might get. At some point we fell fast to sleep. But I am a light sleeper and any noise out of being natural I would become awake. This night was uneventful. We were in very high   spirits   and   tired.

Chapter 7 - Day 5th
July 8, 1985

We awoke to a rainy day drizzly day. Cool, cloudy forecast. (Red sky's in the morning sailors take warning, red sky's at night sailors delight.) This will not be a very good day to be traveling. Besides that Dan was coming down with a cold. I made a shelter to keep our cooking fire dry then made pancakes for breakfast. It was decided to hold up one day. Dan you stay warm and dry get rested up for tomorrow trying to fight off that cold. We had cold medicine and aspirin, to fight the oncoming cold. I stayed outside working on tomorrow's trail flagging it. I took the opportunity of this rainy day to replenish our water supply. This I did before I went off to flagging the trail.

In front of the tent I made a lien too support, for a time I had Dan's help doing this. We used our poly film over this making a surface area of 15 feet by 8 feet sloping. This worked pretty well the water run down to a basin a continued extension of this same poly sheeting. Then again sent Dan back into the tent to keep warm for the rest of the day, I started the way ahead hacking out the brush and marking trail. Marking trail was more than one reason, one for Dan to find me in case I didn't come back. The trail now could be fallowed from the lake on past this camp. It was a cold and wet day, the high end of the lean too, made for a good shelter over the small camp fire. With the dry wood we have stacked under the lean earlier gave us a good supply of dry fire wood.

After all this setting up a dry camp, water catch system, I worked the rest of the day blazing the trail ahead. I tried to make good time in going the way of least resistance but there was not much of that.

This black spruce forest was dark, thick and buggy. When it was raining heavy the bugs went under the leaves. Each step on the moss floor or a bump of a leafy bush the mosquitoes swarmed trying to get at me. Not to the extent they could have because not all my repellent had washed off. But they did like my body heat, at times when I would turn to get an alignment, there would be a black cloud of them sizing me up for dinner. Without having covered skin or repellent I could see how a person could go mad. Mosquitoes do not sleep, there active 24-7 but a bright sunny day they do head for the shade. Sun shine, wind and bug repellent are my friends.

After supper, Dan was feeling better. The warm food, bed rest medicine keeping warm must've helped. Obviously a strenuous workout both of us had has taken its toll. We must travel slow and easy as not to burn out. We had days and a lot of miles yet to travel, we must remain vigilant, to adapt to all situations that may arise.

.

Chapter 8 - Day six
July 9th 1985

Morning sunlight was streaming through the forest tops. Fog and dew all over but the birds were singing. This would mean a new wonderful day. We had done the right thing by holding up a day. It was like we were being watched over or something. Then the rain was gone we could pack away our rain gear. That would be our rain jackets are leggings were stored away at the Lake.

Pancakes again, then we took down the tent. The tent had become heavier due to the rain; we had no time to the dry it. Checking on the water that had collected, I asked Dan. What do you think? Filling the canteens should not be a problem. Boy! I'll say there must be 30 gallons of water there and all pure drinking water too. No water tablets needed. That poly sheeting all 11 pounds, sure glad we brought it with Dad it paid for itself just using it one time. One by one Dan filled up the canteens with his canteen cup. We also drank a lot of water feeling like a camel readying for a trip.

What we do with the rest of it Dad? That fire pit will be used as soon as it is cold out for a place to lay in a cut off a sheet of the poly pour in the water fold it over and cover with heavy timber. Making it hard and out of sight then cover moss over that. We will not count on it, but it would be nice if we had to return this way just a safety precaution then we will most likely never see it again the scouts must always be prepared. I call this campsite "rainy day camp". Well Dan! Are you ready to move out? We should be up on a hill by the end of this day; then we can see some landmarks and check your progress on the map.

This is moose country for sure covered with willow; the ground is covered with moose nuggets like a barnyard. Up on this hill there is a breeze giving them some relief from mosquitoes and good grazing. There was lots of sign of all kinds of animals up here. Back in the forest we come upon a pine squirrel pine cone cache of 10 feet in diameter and some 4 feet high. This was a feeding, collecting, storing area.

The cones were harvested before the cones were dry, while yet green the squirrels pilled them up to dry in one place then in the winter month's peel and eat the seeds, husking and leaving the husk to build up. In these piles of pine cone husk would be escape routes and burros for the squirrel. The pile is built up amongst several smaller trees that make it hard for a bear to dig very fast after a squirrel. Look up into the tree Dan. Nice comfy nest that's a squirrel's home. This spot is his comfort zone.

He has escape routes and trees to climb, a big dinner pile of pine cones he is not in fear of being caught as much here as he would be in other places. That's one old squirrel there are many generations of his family and by the looks of it compared to the time put into it. More than a few times a bear has tried to dig after that squirrel by the looks of how the pile has been knocked down and spread about. This is one determined squirrel. We moved on and somewhere on the line, Dan asked me to hurry up. You're always checking that compass sometimes every 50 feet. You're right Dan, this is a new country to me it would not be hard to get turned around. I cannot see landmarks to go by. Most the time we were in heavy cover and we can't see but that would change in time.

On that point Dan we need to get some landmarks bearings. I sure would like to know where I am; climb that black spruce tree Dan.

Tell me what landmarks you might see. Point me out some hills on this map then I can locate our position on the map. It has been two days now, we could be anywhere. We've been just on a heading in the general direction all this time. Okay Dad up I go. This tree was a big black spruce with a shallow root system so he had to be careful, you know the ground was covered with the mosses that would be good to fall on or have the tree come down too. I could see the ground cover moving. Be careful Dan. that does not have much of a root system, only the moss and spread out roots are keeping the tree up a good wind could bring it down, it has no tap root. Carefully Dan made his way upward, the tree swayed slightly towards Dan.

Dan was as close to the top of the tree it would allow. Then I shouted out! "What do you see?" He answered back, "taller trees." The forest was to flat and only other trees could be seen. Dan was down, sorry Dad but I could not see anything more than taller trees. That's okay you tried at least the tree is still standing and your safely down. Looked a little wobbly there, we will remain on this compass heading at least we have a compass we could be going in circles without it. At this time of the year it is hard to know the direction by looking at the sun. Some time we will be able to figure where we are at. Then we pushed on.

Nearly 18 hours had past today when we broke out on top. This is good Dan I feel like a human, not being able to see far is not for me. Even if I can only see the opposite shore line, that's still not good enough for me. Give me a valley, miles and miles of air to breath. From here we were able to see the Earths horizons in the hazy distance. From here we triangulated off of Haystack Mountain and Bear Paw Mountain using our compass and topographic maps. (No GPS for me in 1985) At last we had us marked on the map.

We are at this point Dan. See that long flat hill off in the hazy distance pointing to it? Looking over several valleys between, that is our destination. That's a long ways, Dad. How far? Laying out the big map measured the distance showing Dan how this was done. 30 miles Dan, that's map miles or air miles, not walking miles up down around zigzag will be a lot more. Then out of nowhere there was a long clearing with few trees. It was out of place not normal. The moss was thin; bed rock could be felt as I walked. Dan said come quickly! He was to my right front looking at the ground. What do you make of this? Barely exposed I could see white rock. Quartz Dan! With our boots, army entrenching spade we scraped more off. Found a wide vain of quartz mixed with gray to black rock. Hand me the metal detector. Setting it adjusting it, turned it on, holding the loop enclosed pad over the surface and moved it side to side like you would do when sweeping a floor not touching the rock. Immediately the detector went ZZZZ-ZZZ-ZZ noisily loud with the needle pegging off the meter. Holy Cow! Dan said. Let me try that! It did the same thing. Okay Dan let me work this over mapping it. It was about 4 feet wide and run on past 100 yards continuing on into the thin black spruce cover. I could not see any greenish tint in the quartz itself, but the quartz was mixed with a large amount of lead gray material.

With the entrenching spade and hand axe we pried out a chunk of the gray about the size of a bread pan, or like a big long box of cheese. Then broke a corner off the gray rock, the exposed color was lighter not as black as the air exposed surfaces were, but a lighter gray. With two hands I handed the big hunk to Dan to hold. Dan nearly dropped it. That's heavy!

Heaver then a normal rock of that size Dad! Yeah it is like 100 pounds Dan. Put it in your pack so you can haul it out with us Dan? You're funny Dad. No way, but maybe a part okay? We marked this spot on the map and piled up a rock pile 4 feet high, a claim with our names dated in a tinfoil bag in the center of this claim. I went on and told Dan this was hard rock silver ore or what is known as galena a mix of all sorts of minerals and lead. That is why it is so heavy for its size. Remotely located now we moved on and some day will return.

We then set camp even though it was late the sun was brightly shinning. Being up high on solid rock, covered with thin moss, with a view overlooking the vast wilderness and enough water in our canteens, this would be a fine place to rest. Even a house or cabin but for now what an advantage point! While I built the rock enclosed fire pit or alter as I called a stone camp fire place. Dan went off with the 22. Rifle leaving his pack at camp, I have the urge for fresh meat Dad. Bring your signal whistle and keep an eye on where you are at all times, this is new country you could become lost.

Resting without carrying a pack was so relaxing. Gathering fire wood I heard a shot. Good I thought, one shot usually means a kill. Then in a few moments another then another Dan was still hunting. Three shot close to gather would be a distress signal. I listened for that. These shots were sporadic. After a time of hearing all the shooting I assumed Dan was target practicing. Knowing we had 500 bullets or what is known a brick. We had an ample amount of bullets but it was not necessary for practicing on this hike.

I thought of things and how to tell Dan when he returned on informing him to keep his shooting to a limit and for need only. I got over Dan's shooting and enjoyed the moment, loosing myself in thoughts. This has to be the ultimate Father Son's wilderness experience of any one's life. Most parents would only be telling of their experiences to their children or grandchildren. We were doing this together; I felt proud beaming a smile from ear to ear. Then too, I was aware that a lot lay ahead, so saved composure for later, much later, now looking into the distant haze of the horizon miles and days ahead.

I shot them Dad! You get to cook them. Dan said, as he made his way over the top and into camp. Yeah sure I said. What were you shooting at? Dan then dropped 12 Bohemian Cedar Wax Wings to the ground. (They are small song birds). Well I'll be darn! They were the size of robins. We're eating fresh meat tonight Dad! We have never eaten small birds before but right now they looked good.

I will always remember Dan's broad smile while he fried the birds. They were so good we ate the bones too. Never again will I question how many times you fire a gun Dan. This meal made our day complete then turned in and Dan went about killing the mosquitos inside the tent with a bit of a pic.

Chapter 9 - Day 7, July 10th, 1985

How many miles do you think we will get today Dad? We were looking at the distant horizon? We have some high ground ahead, but a couple of Valley crossings too then there's the alder thickets at the base of the hills, that will slow us down. Conservatively, I would say five or 6 miles.

Can I take the lead take today? Maybe I can set a faster pace. Sure Dan from here we have to take this ridge in that direction, till it drops off. Then down over and up to that higher ridge follow that to another down and up that 1700 foot hill. See them from here; I'll try to keep up with it you.

That's that Dan, proudly led the charge, we are off an away. We had gone only 150 feet and again we were in the woods. A little while later headed up a slight rise. Nearing the top, Dan called out to me. Dad I have something to show you. What's that? Dan was pointing, looks man made Dan. It is a tripod made of tree poles about 12 feet high. Whatever it was it has been here a long time by the looks of the wood. Upon reaching the tripod up close then I recognize for what it was.

It's a survey Monument Marker, the wood pole tripod was built over the monument for later location. An army helicopter survey crew did this when they mapped Alaska placing one every 6 miles making a 6 square mile township. It is a brass 2 foot long rod anchored with a rounded button head on top just above the surface about three and a half inch in diameter. On it will be the North South, East West lines 4 town ship junctions of corners. The date it was placed, elevation Lat. Long, surveyors work from this in surveying whatever needs to be survived. A helicopter using a known map locates the one that is the closest for a survey project.

On this it was dated: and done by the "The Army Corp of Engineer Company of 1942," then with a knife we carved our names and date (7/10/85) on this brass button too. This brass stake and pole tri pod is as old as I am Dan I was born in 1942. This is a historic site, were most likely the first people here since the army map builders were here in 42.

When Dan and I were finished, Dan took point again. In this area there were a lot of well used moose trails. One was headed off in our direction, Dan fallowed this moose path. The most moose sign I have ever seen was here, it was like a barn yard of paths good dry ground but wet enough for the willows. The paths worked their way around the willows like it was a garden of feeding stations, the moose kept these trimmed back like gardener pruning his trees, not eating the trees to the nubbin but harvesting only the succulent new growth.

Moose foot prints were the size of elephants and not one but several. To hunt and harvest moose here would take a big helicopter I would estimate one would be an easy 2,000 pounds after field dressing. No one drops a moose even a small one any distance from a river or land able lake. These moose were safe from man and I am sure any pack of wolves had great respect for them. One hour had past and we have not dropped down to the valley. Dad! Dad! Look another tri pod pointing at it. Knowing we had not travelled 6 miles, a weak feeling came over me..... Dan! Read the button. When he did, the look of astonishment was on his face as well as his body language looked limp. How can that be? How? Dan just could not accept this, his mind was perplexed. I had been fallowing Dan's heels, bent over just fallowing moving right along behind keeping up.

We had for one hour travelled in a near full twisted circle. If it had not been for that tripod, manmade land mark, we might yet be living off the land lost for ever and ever, so it felt at that moment. We had been lost for an hour and did not know it. Dan you just had lesson in getting lost. Could have been worse we might have been confused for a day or so but not lost then I laughed out loud. But how the sun is up there, not a cloud, I went straight? Dan asked. Well Dan, this is Alaska in July, sure the sun is shining but this time of the year it is straight up or nearly.

Then as you made your way, traveling a path of least resistance instead of aligning land marks even from tree to tree a straight line or checking a compass AHEM! You weaved twisted and made a straight line for an hour with a slight curve in it, like Earth. Keep going straight west from here you would end up here. I think that is how someone figured out this planet is round. Notice how you favoured your right and not going down any? Well some instincts we best not fallowed. We're fortunate we came back to this tri pod. Lesson well learned. Like a person with a hangover, Dan remained confused completely befuddled.

Guess I will take point at least for a while. Now you know why I check my compass often. I was not hard on him and no more was said. Dan was going to have to take time to recover from this himself unravelling his own puzzle. I turned his attention to the matters at hand. Not one cross word was said between us this had been a true test of a relationship between a Son and Father.

The mosquitoes were bad all the times but less on the tops of hills and in the sun. Never were we completely free of them, there annoying sounds of continues bussing was maddening, thankfully we had the repellent and protective clothing to cover as needed. Thanks too for the times in the tent. Dan had it down pat on killing those trapped inside.

On one rest stop we found us a bench log seat and a supporting rest for our packs to remain on. This day I tested myself on how black my leg could get by seeing how many mosquitoes could land, drill and pump on my one leg from my knee up that had no repellent. Dan watched as it was not long before that not a 1/8 of an inch was between them blood pumping drill rigs.

Dan just shook his head and said Dad there full now. So they are, watch this, with one hand I plowed them flat smooching them dead. DANG! Dad that must have hurt! Yes it did but now I have a red pants leg, let's not do that again. It was time to apply more repellent. Put this pitcher in your mind, one zillion sucking big mosquitoes all pumping at one time.

High noon temperatures reached 100 degrees added to the discomfort having to be well covered meant even more of a slow pace. Not to have been prepared for this Alaskan jungle wilderness adventure this hike would never have happen. The winters are the best time for travelling before the ice becomes unsafe and the time when there are no mosquitoes flying about. June through Mid-August was the worst months.

Now we are descending down off the ridge we're on, down to a thick jungle of swamp, bogs only to climb another hill. Relatively free of trees, as to that reason why there are fewer trees on this side is greatly due to the fact that the snow remains here for longer periods of time being sheltered from the sun and the two foot of moss over frozen ground or bed rock. It was on this hillside we refilled our canteens.

There was a small gully with snow melt and ice melt flowing with ice cold water.

Most likely this water was safe to drink but flowing through the mosses but to be sure we put one tablet per quart of water to purify it just to be safe. Then shake the canteens not stirred, and then wait a few minutes before drinking. The water then tastes like medicine but the germs if any in the water are killed. Saves time by not having to set up a fire and bring the water to a rolling boil for 20 minutes.

My prior experience of hiking in remote Alaska and the longest time on my own was a week during a month of July. [In writing this account of this hike, it is not my intent to shock, make you gasp; give any false impressions but to make you the reader informed as to the risks and how important it is to be prepared. Hopefully you are enjoying our wilderness adventure that is not within a park but better than a park, that has no well-used paths, garbage containers, asphalt, tables, benches, trimmed trees, closing hours, signs, or planes flying overhead, only utter pure wilderness of true Alaska.

We continued on down the hillside. Slowly, deliberately, with caution, the tundra layered with thick covered moss concealed many obstacles that could cause us to stumble or even break a leg. Now on the bottom we were at the base of the next hill, there was heavy enclosed under growth to wiggle through, alder trees being the worst of the entanglements. No thorns just a low lying sprawled clustered mass of shrubs. Where ever a limb touched the ground cover it would take root and sprout a new tree adding to the mass of entangled puzzle. We had to find a way through before gaining an upward assent. There is pink alder heart wood and white alder heart wood. There is no difference on the outside. They all look the same till you cut deep to the heart wood.

Then you will see the color. I like the pink wood for carving. My guess is one is a male the other is a female alder. This was the time we used the east wing hand axe to chop our way through. (Alder trees are of the birch family.) The chopping was done; we were now in a mix of white birch and spruce. No more crawling and chopping, pulling or pushing.

It helped being in the dark woods, as far as temperatures', but still had to keep on the head nets, gloves, and light jackets protecting us from the hordes of mosquitoes. Hot being sweaty made for us to drink a lot of water, water is like oil and water to a machine, you never want to run low on water. Water is the most important ingredient in the human body.

The light from the top of the hill now could be seen. Not much further Dan, the going will become easier soon. When we reach the top we will have to go to right to the northeast taking the openings on the higher ground to the end of the ridge line probably about 3 miles long.

It was a good feeling again to be on top where we could see. On the top the moose seemed to be enjoying this area too. More trails were everywhere but this time we checked the compass often, even though the trail may look like it was going the right way. We would have to be sure. Making good time we reach near where we wanted to drop down. This area had a lot of square rock, black basalt making for good building stone.

At this point before we'd drop down again into a messy terrain I had a decision to make. If we went on with our days march we would be somewhere down there in that jungle. And I did not, favor that idea. I would rather stop here and press forward tomorrow.

Dan was all for camping near this high rocky hilltop. As a father son team we quickly set up camp. This whole journey was all about teamwork. There never was a harsh word spoken between us we had mutual respect. There was a real effort on my part sometimes to show confidence and have a convincing positive attitude at all times. After all we were into this journey together to have doubts or show panic is not in the plan. Dan had a lot of questions like, how far, when, if's, and are we going to have to walk out?

So I always had a good answer, mainly to reinstate his confidence in me. Even though, all his questions asked I didn't truly know the answer myself at times. Some obstacles had to be confronted first then the answer would come to me. Of this I was always sure. For I believe we had a guardian angel guiding us on this journey. I knew how to listen to my sixth sense, to search my feelings for the answer.

Even though we were camped out in the open, the mosquitoes were very bad at this site for the lack of wind. It seemed to be we were making camp during the time of the day when, it was the hottest. Then getting underway early in the cool morning hours was the best. I want to add something about mosquito head nets. There is no need for camouflaged head nets they make it very difficult to see out of.

That was one mistake that I made. I wore a camouflage head net on this hike. It was the hardest thing to see through and very unsafe. Dan had a very unique way of killing mosquitoes trapped inside his head net. He would simply inhale them and swallow with a kind of evil glee in his eyes.

Daniel had this perfected by opening his mouth, if the mosquitoes did not fly in; he would just draw in air as they hovered in front of his mouth. It was his way of getting even, perhaps, or maybe he was trying to recapture some of his blood. Or maybe one too many bit him in the head. In any case it was a way to make light of the otherwise horrible annoying situation.

Being bitten by mosquitoes in Alaska, so far there are no mosquito caring illnesses or diseases such as malaria or sleeping sickness. The only thing to fear is being eaten alive, which could happen by the mosquitoes here in Alaska. They are big as birds. Whatever you do don't let one land on each shoulder picking you up and carry you away.

From camp we could look back to where our last camp was. Far short of 5 to 6 miles 4 maybe at best no more. Turning in for the night Dan had fun killing the remaining mosquitoes within the tent.   We're running low on water Dad! Okay, there should be more, less than 1 mile

Chapter 10 - Day 8, July 11th, 1985

It was going to be another hot day, dry weather was better than being wet so we were not complaining. After a pancake breakfast, the tent was taken down, rolled up, loaded up and we moved on. It was a slow descent traveling downward angling along the steep hillside then north again becoming relatively open. The ground was covered, with moss and rotting wood. Walking over thick moss was always like walking on a coil spring mattress with lumps very springy but surprising. In the beginning of the hike we both wore brand-new jungle Vietnam, combat boots. It gave us good traction, ankle support, and canvas reinforced that drained water. Stress and strain on my boots traveling through this tundra moss took a toll. At the bottom found something to sit on. I had to remove my left boot.

What's the problem Dad? That steep hillside walk ripped out the side of my boot right by the arch where the reinforced canvas is joined to the bottom. Dan do you have the backpack cord? Yup! Coming right up Dad! This cord was a roll of carpenters chalk line. I used a length of this cord to hold the upper part of the shoe to the bottom rubber sole before it became worse. Sure glad we brought that cord.

The hill we were about to climb now was 1700 feet. Going around would have been shorter. But the jungle at its base would take us two days. Growing on this hill was large, white spruce of massive size. Ideal for house logs, enough timber to build a log home. Again, the going was tough a lot of chopping wiggling climbing over fallen trees or crawling under. Eventually we were clear. We were now in the clear and gained some distance. We could now rest a bit knowing what was behind us. Going up and over looked a lot easier, instead of continuing on around. It was then I noticed my $23 East wing leather bound hand axe was missing. The holster was busted. Turns out the cases were made rather cheaply, well made for normal use but not for this trip.

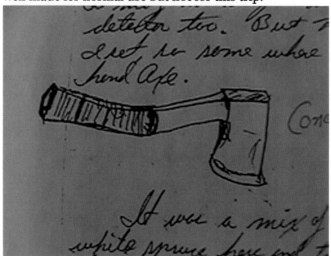

The axe was top of the line but the case wasn't up to this hard of a hike. I removed my pack and made tracks back a ways just in case it was near. Not wanting to spend much time looking it, it might never be found even in a day, I used the metal detector too. It could be found but time was treasure so I turned back.

So somewhere out there is a fine east wing hand axe. This was a lesson to be visual of our inventory that hung on us. For the first time we were not on rock but a silt beneath the moss. It was like dust, gray color but abrasive like fine polishing dust. Then upon further examination come to the conclusion it was volcanic ash. I never took the time to dig down but assumed there was a stone hill under this ash as per the hills we have been over up to now. We were on the edge of an ash storm or of an ash fall out. No wonder why the trees looked healthier in this area they had a better root system and drainage. That is why the birches and white spruce mix. Black spruce liked the wetter areas.

The climb was going well only the hill was the task and foot holds, it was steep at times holding on to a tree pulling myself up. Dan was some distance ahead in sight yet but was doing great in leading the way forging a route. By now we had made some good distance up, Dan turned and said I see the top Dad, there's light ahead. Can't be Dan this is the highest hill around are you sure? Yup! It is rounding and the tree tops are thinning. Then like a Marine about to plant a flag he got a burst of energy and scrambled up on out of sight. Shortly I heard a loud groan and an Oh! NO! Rats! I made my way up to Dan. The disappointing body language Dan had was understandable. We were not at the top but only a setback of a shelf on the hill. We had all of what we had climbed in height yet to do. The makeup of the forest was the same only a flat distance before we were back on the steep hill with no day light or sign of the top in sight.

Again we pushed on upwardly; again Dan saw the light and hurried forward. Once again another level and a hill, after 3 times sure, maybe 5 times before we, finally summited the top. But just to be sure I sent Dan on ahead; he came back and said, WERE HERE! Because of the tree cover we could only see to our west and north. But we knew where we were this was the 1700 foot elevation marked hill marked on the map and small in diameter on top. To the west was the Kuskokwim Mountain range. It looked near but baron of life. To the north basically was the way we were headed, looked green and full of life. Open Country Dan loudly proclaimed! Open country meant no trees only grasses let me have a look Dan. Maybe over there but were not headed that way. Rats Dan said. Then I pointed out our route.

Another jungle huh Dad! Looks like it Dan; plus some swamps this time. We have to cross that vast bottom to get to those hills way yonder. At least part of the trip will be easier. Yeah! I'm headed down, Dan said. Traveling down was almost fun but of course that kind of thinking could get you into trouble there for continued carefully on down but quicker, with less work and effort. Drinking water was short so we headed for any kind of a clue as to where we would come across a water source on our way down. Dan was the first to hear running water.

It was hidden from view but it was getting louder telling us we were close. It seemed to be coming down a narrow groove or cut on the side hill. Dan honed in on the sound of gushing water like a heat seeking missile. Then there it was coming right out of a stone wall shooting out nearly two feet with pressure. The artesian water was a 2 inch flow then falling some 8 feet to a basin and spilling over running out from that point. This stream of water as barely above freezing temperature and never varied in the force. By the looks of it, it has been flowing here since the beginning of time. This was on the dark side of the mountain and 8 feet above the floor. This 1700 mountain held or trapped the water in its belly and like a leak spewed forth from solid rock this stream like in the Bible. This flowing water could make power and supply a home for ever.

The water was the best I have ever tasted no stink only clear cold pure water. I would someday like to revisit this site. Sadly I did not take a photo of the flowing stream of water but you can see the level ground it landed and dispersed. This flowing force was concealed behind thick shrubs and trees. I would have had to do a lot of clearing for a good photo in hind sight I should have tried. This water made a refreshing washing stop cold, too cold for an all over bath but the cool air lessoned the mosquitoes letting us remove the head nets. It was very invigorating washing in ice cold water and brushing our teeth.

Dan even shampooed his hair looking all pretty again for whom I do not know but he felt belter. The back packers signal mirror was used. We had the running water just needed the sink. Dan even endured the cold flowing water pouring on his head rinsing the shampoo out. I would have gotten a brain freeze. Dan just grinned and smiled, Dan would be one that would laugh in the face of evil.

Dad! Dan said. What? Dad, the right side of your head looks like raw hamburger. Then with the mirror I inspected and with my hand felt the damaged temple side of my head. What had happened was apparent. My head net had been up against my temple and the mosquitos had their way with me. Because of my head wound the whole right half of my head is paralyzed, so I had not felt a thing.

The damage was serious and needed to be tended to or infection would take over. It was a 2 inch area of bloody raw flesh. First aid time Dad! We treated it like a burn applying burn ointment after thoroughly washing with that cold clean running water. Guardian angel is with us Dad. Thankfully I did not feel the cold water. This self-flowing water was truly a blessing. Had this raw flesh not been found now here, it could very well become infected? Thanks too to being prepared with a full medical kit. From this point forward in our hike we made sure our head nets did not come close to skin for the mosquitoes to drill through.

Resting for a time we then filled up on water by drinking our fill filled the canteens and moved on to complete the day. It was always a hard go in the bottoms this day would be no different. Traveling top the hills and ridges was the way to travel. Then an opening a space of light begins to appear we then went towards it like moths to a flame. Well look at that Dad! Neat huh! It was a marsh with tall water grass; it looked like a jungle marshy lagoon pond deep within the woods. This hidden lagoon was an eerie feeling to be standing at its edge. It was like we had went back in time two million years.

We see ghosts of plant eating dinosaurs, expecting any moment to see a monster raise its head above the grassy misty haze lagoon. This lagoon had a solid bank rim, so with a long pole I probed it pushing down 16 feet and no bottom was felt. I think this is a warm spring Dan that never freezes. Alaska is known for hot springs, there not always hot but might never freeze over. I am sure this is one. Wish I had the time and equipment to drag the depths for bones. I am sure there is a treasure trove of history down there. From the air flying over this it might never be seen, were very fortunate Dan to come across this. The water detour time Dad! Yup! Luckily this was a contained round lagoon not a lake sized one. We can walk around this. Let's hope we do not come to a big marsh to go around. Were still in the jungle using a compass to guide our way not fun but at times can be very interesting indeed. I hear running water Dad! Good, on the map there's a creek ahead so we're making some headway. The creek had running water but was so filled in covered over with fallen trees we could walk over it on the dead falls.

It was a trench size rushing creek, the kind that would disappear under the ground and under growth. Dan was far ahead of me, I lingered crossing over this treacherous creek having a heavy pack things could quickly go wrong, like falling upside down getting trapped in the water and drown. Then an urgent call came from Dan. When hiking in the wilderness urgent calls could mean life or death, none of this huh! What? Why? I guess, are you sure? Responsive timely reactions could save a life. Dad! Hurry up! Come quick! A thousand thoughts ran through my mind as I hurriedly moved towards Dan. He looked okay! But what was he standing in?

Is it a clearing? Dad... What is this? It's a bloody miracle that is what it is Dan. Several years ago a big caterpillar dozer with wide track pads, for winter traveling for traveling over any soft low warm areas. It was probably in the month of March while the days were long and the ground yet hard. It might have been as long ago as 1942 that air strip on Lake Minchumina was built by a caterpillar dozer Dan.

It would have had to have been walked in well over a 150 miles way back when. From where I could only guess. Somewhere from the parks High Way or the Kuskokwim is my guess. Then only in places did the under growth reclaimed the trail it made. Traveling in the winter there would have been no real damage to the country side except for the trees it pushed over. In any case Dan there is truly a guarding angel watching over us. What do you mean Dad? Well look at this for a moment.

The track pads packed down a path coming from the way were headed and only by chance you came on to this after the willows behind us grew back in concealing the trail forever that had been made perhaps 45 to 50 years ago. More than likely this trail too ahead be closed back in, we found a piece of history again Dan. Thank You God now looking up, we could have been off by 20 feet or less and never seen this. Now let's make use of the time this will save.

We fallowed this Cat trail for a long ways taking us through some of the thickest low lying thickest of the hike, the 2 foot wide pads of what must have been a D-8 caterpillar dozer with extra wide size pads. The imprints were clearly seen as it if they were made 2 days ago but clearly the grown back in trees and shrubs were all of 40 years old.

Plus the dozed trees had rotted away 30 years ago those that fell all the way to the ground, some were still hanging dry hanging up against other trees. The pressed in tracks were used by the moose and they were keeping this open by eating the willows trimming them human shoulder or head high and only had to chew the new growth tips on either side of the two paths, one track more used then the other being 8 feet apart. The moose favoured one more than the other probably due to more wood to eat on one side verses the other track. The cat trail broke into a very large area of about 260 acres of meadow and hassocks.

This open area could have been a snow dragged flat for an otter air plane to land or a big chopper, I would suspect was used to resupply the machinery with fuel, food and other needs a cat train would have needed when being pulled along with the caterpillar to doze the air field during WW2 during the early 40's. Some year to come there will be a road from some point on the parks highway south of Nenana through here to Minchumina on to Nome Alaska thus opening up Alaska for easier access to minerals and its growing population. Maybe even a rail road on to Russia.

It was time to find a place to make camp but where? This was a hassock and wet land no man's land, it was the course I had set we had to cut across some of it. Hassocks' or hummock's and there is another slang term used for them too, much of this and I will have a name for them too.

There marsh plants grasses that grow in a Colum standing in water on permafrost under the water. Hummocks are a hiker's night mare they cannot be stepped on unless one is of large diameter but most are narrow and have to be straddled or walked around in no pattern but a big maze. This area seemed to be the home for sparrow hawks that lived on rodents and weasels. The problem we had was it was nearing 2 o'clock in the morning day light yet but barely. We needed to find a round enough hummock to put our tent and get some sleep. We looked all about for that round spot for the tent. Over here Dad! Not much Dan but it will have to do. The self-supporting tent barely fit on this big hummock. Grasp this picture inside there was a lump in the center that we circled around sleeping in a curve. Outside all night there were noises of water lapping and of moose walking nearby; they made a sucking sound by their big feet sinking in and pulling lifting them up to take another. It was music to our ears and we went fast to sleep.

Chapter 11 - Day 9 & 10, July 12th & 13th 1985

This morning of July 12th Dan said not your perfect camp site huh? No but it might make a good duck blind. We had entered into a new kind of valley more open than any before, some hummocks, dead dry black spruce barren of limbs. Apparently the ground had been too wet and the spruce that had grown died leaving only the poles killdeer birds favoured this country. Not much happening today and made maybe 8 miles, it was one of our better days.

At the days end we set camp on a sand bar of a small creek with spruce trees on the banks, the place where there was drainage for better growing trees. The tundra was to wet and looked like it had been burned off several years ago no dead wood on the ground it had rotted away of what there had been, only a few dead poles stood.

The near dry sand bar made for a good camp site no worries of a camp fire getting out of control and water right close before we put the tent up I showed Dan how to make shallow pockets for our hips because there was no moss to bed down on here. Good Idea Dad! Experience Dan, experience! Stick with me and you will learn.

After supper we looked back to review the way we had come. We had come a long ways. This was no hill top but we could see a long distance in every direction. We had typical camp fire talks of our trek and everything that we had overcome. Dan was now becoming a veteran hiker.

We had a long ways to go yet but competently now with continued caution we would be fine. Thinking the night was over we turned in. (Ready for this?) Our night's sleep was rudely interrupted about 2 A.M., we were soundly sleeping.

Dad! Dad! Is that you? I awoke with a lurch. "SHUT UP I AM TRYING TO GET SOME BLAKE-de-BLAKE-SLEEP DANG IT" Then rolled over and went back to sleep so did Dan. In the morning the upper most on my mind was, of Dan waking me up last night.

Was he having a bad dream or what? I had to ask. Dan about last night sorry I yelled at you. That's okay Dad. Whatever it was your loud angry voice chased it off. What do you mean? Well I was sound asleep when I awoke. Something was pushing me from the outside of the tent. I was pushed over a good six inches. I thought it was you. When you answered my question I got real scared but only for a moment. Because whatever was pushing me didn't want anything to do with you and it went away. I then went back to sleep.

My eye brows raised, let's check this out we are on a sand bar there should be tracks. "HOLY COW"! We both exclaimed! Dan, my son, your very lucky you were visited by --- by the size of these tracks --- "A BIG MEAN GRIZZLEY BEAR" maybe so Dad but you're meaner and laughed. The paw prints were 6.5 inches wide by 10.5 inches long with 3 inch claws extending from the toes. This Grizzly had nuzzled Dan over then heard my loud angry voice and run off.

Leaving the creek we had to travel through a low wide side hill that drained into the creek. The way was looking to be an easy walk. Dan was in the lead moving right along when he said, Dad what's this? Seems to be an old creek filled in with moss but further investigating it was not a creek. It was a long mossy wet watery super saturated with low moss and algae growth with short grasses like you might see in old unattended livestock tank. This was any ware from 8 to 16 feet wide with an occasional small black spruce tree on a clump of a firmer growth of moss. There were no trees in this area, had there been even one we could have used it by laying it over and cross this narrow down slopping swamp in open country not a normal wet spot. At first glance it looked like not much of an obstacle and could be a wet crossing is all.

Going around would mean up to at least a mile going right or left. It was like looking over crevasse to jump across and be on our way. Dan wanted to charge across this, he was not afraid of getting a little wet. Holding Dan back was like trying to hold a horse that smelled water after a long dry spell on the range. This was not your normal wet spot. Poking it with a slender pole found it to be "QUICK SAND" with no bottom at least for me. It was all thick stinking sucking muck. That's that Dan we have to go around. But that will mean hours Dad!

Sorry Dan but You do not cross quick sand. I was ready to walk around going higher up where it should end. Then I see a movement from the corner of my eye in this muck. I train my eye looking for what it was. There were small holes in the thin moss of 1 inch diameters here and there. I had not noticed before. Watch Dan there's something living in them. We stood still then a small snake about 10 inches long slither fast on into another hole. Then in another spot a 2nd, it had a round head not blunt telling me it most likely had no fangs like a rattler would. I saw 3 in all and they moved swiftly extremely fast darting like, all were short from 8 to 10 inches.

Reddish in color the color could have come from the muck they lived in. Then wondered how could a snake be living here in the center of Alaska in such a cold climate? Then I put my hand in this mucky water quick sand and it was warm. For sure not cold like other wet spots or streams. That explained to me a lot they had their own warm environment. (Had I known there are no snakes in the center of Alaska I would have captured one and put my name on the species)

Now back to the task at hand. (Where is the film crew? This would have been good for a movie of what was to fallow) Dan found a narrow place with a small tree in the center, a clump. Let me try Dad. Take your pack off come here. I tied the rope some 50 feet long we had, under his arms. I could have ordered Dan to follow me around this quicksand seep but there are some things in life that are best learned the hard way. All the same I was not about to lose my son in this lesson. (I hope to tell you how this looked to me to you the reader.)

Dan took his first step sunk some right off but not bad, then his next step sunk more but yet okay. Each move forward he sunk more, now well over his knees.

It was like seeing Dan walking down steps, each an 8 inch step. Can you feel bottom? No only mushy muck, turn back Dan. Give it up. I can make it Dad I am nearly to that tree. Dan at every move was sinking faster and struggling just to move. (Ever see quick sand at work?) It is not pretty. Dan now turned back facing me, up to his arm pits and was stuck yet sinking.

Dan was out of reach but thank you lord he had a rope under his arms. I was not quick in pulling him out the lesson was not done. Dan looked up at me still sinking inch by inch. His arms were now hugging the mucks surface and soon would take him all the way. That's when he said. PULL DAD! Then again almost in a panicky voice, PULL NOW, NOW! Dan was anchored well in fact pulling him was like an anchor that was stuck on the bottom. He held fast to the rope and I pulled with all my might. Slowly like pulling out a fence post he was moving up leaning then like a water skier coming up on top he was out on top and I drugged him to solid ground.

PEEUEE! You stink something God awful Dan. Dan had that smile from ear to ear glad to be back on solid ground. Well Dad, I learned a new lesson today. That you did, that you did Dan. Now though run on back to the creek, jump in cloths and all you are rotten bear bait, I will wait here and look for more snakes.

It was frustrating to Dan on how long a narrow gradual slopping seeping wet spot could stop our progress but now with this experience we walked around, way around! This indeed was an adventurous journey. Off again we went to see what was over the next ridge. The area we were in now, was a dead forest.

A wild fire had left sticks, ashes and tree stumps. Most of the dead fallen trees had rotted away for the most part so this fire had happened a long time ago. Walking was fairly easy but for some rotting logs, weaving in around new growth of trees and bushes. By walking through this old burn we got a good look at what this fire had did and behaved.

On the ridge tops we seen where the fire had with force rushed up the sides at the same time like a bond fire coming together forming a point that could be seen by the dead standing wood yet supporting each other the trees died a horrible death. It had been an extremely hot fire of hurricane force.

Nothing was left standing except for the dry dead logs supporting each other at the top not fallen nor completely burned to ash but killed the forest and what lay on the ground rotted. Something most people do not know is that a wild fire does not often burn to ash green trees but only the dry fuels, killing the green trees to fall and rot latter. Controlled fires done during early damp mornings with no wind and weather service reports, is a good thing to keep the dead fuels burned saving a forest. Back fires are done this way to take away the fuels for a fire to feed on and then burning its self out. This photo is of a controlled burn, the photo was taken a week afterwards. It was done at night taking several hours to complete while the humidly was high, not even a breeze and fire fighters snuffing out the fires as the fuels had burned.

The raging on coming out of control wild fire ended when it reached this long line of a man made burned out fire break void of fuel. Looks like we found open country Dan back up on new high ground. Continuing on we crested a higher hill. From this point we had our first good view of our destination. Get out the maps Dan. Using the compass, maps and land marks, we located ourselves once again on the map. Were here and that big lake north of us is here on the map. According to the map we are 8 map miles away from that lake to the left, is of a good size about 1 mile in diameter.

That is our final destination. First we have to check out 3 places to the west of that some 4 miles then to it. We will be coming at it from the back side almost. We're a lot closer than we were July 4th. Packs are lighter too Dad. How we doing on food Dan? It will be close but the berries are out now, a bit green but eatable.

Dad! Look over on the far shore line of that lake. What do you make that out to be? Yeah I see it, there are some 64 claims over there scattered around all the lakes and other places of the 30,000 acres. And there are a number of them on that lake someone should be home. What we're seeing is a structure; appears to be a tall white 20ft Indian lodge. Some day we will be there. YEAH! Dan said.

There will be planes, dogs, kids, boats, cabins and good cooking. From that lake or one of the other 4 we will hop a flight back to Fairbanks. Seeing the end in sight gave us new encouragement to push on with new vigor. We made camp on this high ground that night over looking my new future homestead lord willing and if a spot of land speaks to me. Like a lady Dan the feeling has to be mutual.

Chapter 12 - Day 11, July 14th 1985

The berries were out; we're now eating partly off the land. Most berries were green but to us like green apples they were good. Currents and cloud berries were abundant. Cloud berry is nothing a ground raspberry plant low to the ground with a large leaf. When mature it is red to orange and the size of your thumb. One berry to a plant, these can be found on north moss covered slopes or on the bottom in shaded areas.

Currents are very tasty, the plants grow knee high in clusters the berries hang in a row. They may be found in the sheltered woods on hill sides or most everywhere. There two kinds, one taste bad and I think are poisonous. I call those "SKUNK BERRIES", for the reason they stink bad and are a fuzzy berry, not smooth like the good ones; it is very easy to see the difference. If you pick them to fast you might get them confused as the at first glance they look the same. Check your berry book to be sure I am no expert, but by experience know the difference. My rule is anything that tastes bad it is bad at least for me.

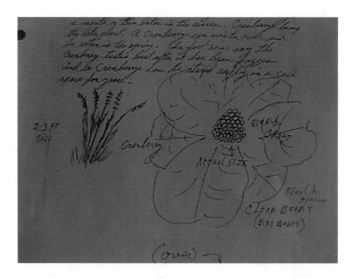

Whenever we could we picked and ate the cloud berries, some areas were abundant with them. One place in particular, I remember was an open north side of a hill, there was no problem eating our fill. Currents, Dan would eat but also store them to eat in the tent for snacks at night. We had run out of raisins for a snack so the currents were a blessing. Also we still had tang and Dan loved to wet his fingers and jam them into the tang and get his tang that way besides in the canteens.

I think tang was a lift for us in drinking on this hike by way of drinking more water. (See! We were not hurting by not having food and treats.) We now had currents each night before we turned in to sleep thanks to Dan. This day was such a day, picking, eating berries as we went but what we needed most was water and traveling on these ridge lines was okay but this one was a long one. Water could be found when going down or at least perhaps ice under the moss in the shaded areas. Up here was dryness and heat but easy to travel.

We were entering an old burn now and it was perhaps the worst thus far. It was at the stage of fallen trees waist high logs lying about above the ground in all directions with the roots up and thick new 2 inch diameter trees growing up through this. That gave it a 3 dimensional gig saw puzzle a day time night mare!

Like bull dozers we put our backs and packs into it forcing our way turning often to climb over or crawl under dead falls. After a time doing this, we came to a small clearing and rested. To drink some water, on reaching for a canteen I said to myself, O CRAP! During this whole hike I had been warning Dan not to lose his large bulky 2 quart canteen he carried by slinging it over his outside framed back pack. (I prefer a Mountain pack for this kind of a hike.) One of my one quart canteens attached securely to my adjustable army utility belt, or so they were till now. To my horror one was now missing. Dan noticed the look on my face and then asked, what's wrong Dad?

Well, first I lost a brand new axe now a canteen full of precious water. NO! You didn't huh Dad? I am afraid so Dan. At that point Dan pointed out to me on how I had been after him to be careful not to lose his canteen. I had two canteens on my belt and Dan had one on his belt plus the big 2 quart hung on his pack. So it was not like we were not prepared but on this hike losing a canteen was to lose preciously needed water. Maybe I can back track and find it! Sure Dad! Do you think you can find the trail we just plowed through? I looked behind me and there was not a clue as to where we had been.

We poked around a bit for a time and called it a lost canteen. We now had to be extremely careful not to over extend our selves on the lack of water. Dan put an extra grip on his big canteen checking the sling. The test of running low on water was not short in coming. We broke out of the tangled maze and now were on top making good time. This ridge was long, very hot well over 100 degrees, no winds, not even a breeze. I was even too hot for the mosquitoes. Water was the up most on our mind not out but dangerously low. The foliage was wilting, dropping limp, on this hill top. Mind you to keep cool we sweated a lot and water had to be replaced frequently to remain healthy and alert. Now where's our guardian angel Dad? We are okay, lots of berries and water enough for today.

We will find water at the end of this ridge as we drop down. We had went for 18 hours on this day again, normally we make camp at water sites but this day by the looks of the map we were yet 2 miles from a possible source. A water source was a line on the topographic map indicating a draw or drainage. It always could be dry only a drainage during wet times.

Topographic maps are blessing to back packers and every hiker should study them well and take them along on the hike keep them from becoming wet and convenient. Now days GPS's make for pin point location at any time. But a good compass should also be in the back packers pack for a backup. In order to use cell phones you need to be within range of a cell tower to work that is about 30 miles.

That night was a dry camp of eating food using no water but for drinking. Then we had berries for desert thanks to Dan leaving a bunch for tomorrow. That night we had our last drink of water. Okay Dan! Here are our options for tomorrow. There are 2. First one is: We could leave our camp set up travel light find water then return. Or 2nd choice:

You stay here in the tent conserve your energy keeping an ear open for 3 shots in case of distress. I will flag, marking my way down the side hill east of where we are now, dropping low find water and returning by noon or there about. Then break camp head north on down to water. It is too hot for a forced march with all we have to carry. I don't like the first choice and not much of the 2nd but it seems the better of the two.

Chapter 13 - Day 12, July 15th 1985

This morning we ate only currents that we had in abundance saving some. The day was clear with a slight breeze we went with plan 2. It had to be done early at the coolest time of the day. Dan it's very important to rest, keep out of the sun remain in the tent. I will mark my trail flagging it well always have 2 flags in view, there will be no guessing to where the trail is. If I have trouble I will fire 3 rounds and wait for your 1 round reply, if there is no reply in timely fashion I will fire again anther 3 rounds. If you have to come for me do not stumble or otherwise get hurt, see you around noon with or without water.

I proceeded on down marking trail, bending my neck looking here; there for any clues of a water source and keeping my ears open for that running gurgling water. I was nearing the half-way point and it was getting difficult in that the jungle was becoming thicker. Half-way point meaning to get back at noon would be close. I am sure there would be water way on down there but the plan was to be back around noon. If I did go all the way it would have been the same as breaking camp and proceeding any way. It was time to turn back to camp.

I worked my way back fallowing my flagged trail; glad I did that saved me in finding my way back. Cresting the hill now, it was some 50 yards to the tent that was looking good in the sun there on the hill top. Dan must have been inside of it.

All I could think was what am I going to tell Dan? We will have to make a forced march and the sooner the better. Not in a big hurry to tell Dan the news yet. I looked around for a place to sit to really rethink on this. This ridge was all rock with very little plant life with some scrub brush. I was near a swale, a shallow dip on the side of this hill. Here I seen what looked like round sofa cushions made of thick moss about 6 feet in diameter and 18 inches high. That looks comfortable, so went over and sat one it.

Sitting down easy, my full weight now on it found it to be very comfortable. Almost immediately my pants became wet. WET! I stood up turned around and thrust my fist deep into it, opened my hand grabbed a hand full and brought it out. The white roots of this moss were dripping wet, not just wet but supper wet. ....WATER! Set up a hanky filter and filled all the canteens full and only a small hole was made in this moss cushion. There had to have been 100 gallons of moss water in that cushion. Tasted of moss but with the water purification tablets and letting them sit after shaking the now full canteens the water was good to drink. To think we were but 50 yards from water all this time. So everyone water can be found on top a hill. Thank You GOD!

With the water, we prepared a late but filling breakfast, loaded up and moved on. I knew I could count on you Dad! I had help Dan, I had help. Our guardian angel is with us. It would be wise for us to continue being careful it is not luck Dan that we have come this far it is the experience we gain each passing day. Life is an adventure and we are fortunate to be living it. Others will learn from us, some may even be inspired to make their own way in life. Be alert, and press on with pride with no regrets.

This long day even with a late start we made a distance of eight miles or longest distance so far. At last we had reached the end of this ridge top, rounding at first then dropping steeply through a thick stand of trees. The sound of fast moving water in the distance spurred us on. It was after midnight and getting darker. HURRY UP DAD! HURRY UP! Dan was following close behind as we went from one tree to the next hands on the trees even steeper now gravity was gaining momentum we were swinging from tree to tree no longer a walk but a monkey dance. The rushing water was even louder we had to be close but no creek was in sight. Reaching the creek would mean the days end and camp set up. We were excited by the sound of rushing water. We were almost free falling we were moving so effortlessly fast. In fact I thought we were moving fast enough when Dan again said. HURRY UP DAD!

SMASH! CRACK! AHH!

Quick as a blink of an eye, I found myself on my back; my body hanging with my arms to my sides draped over fallen trees heals on the ground, white water 6 feet under me. There I was full pack, hat on, shot gun in one hand, metal detector in the other. The creek was a narrow worn cut covered with fallen trees and now me holding on for dear life with my heavy pack weighing me down. If I would fall with my pack on in this deep mountain stream of rushing water I would surely have drowned or at least come close to it. The dry dead tree of 4 inch diameters were creaking and cracking, like telling me we can't hold you much longer. I felt the trees were getting ready to dump me into this foreboding drown able stream. Dan was there laughing his butt off. I did not see the humor in this at all.

"THIS IS ANOTHER FINE FIX YOU GOT ME INTO". Stop Laughing and pull me out of this. I was helpless the full heavy pack was pulling me down bit by bit, a crack and creak at a time. My hands were full, my hat was still on. If I fell in this fashion it would be bad news, head could get smashed on a rock, get tangled under water, pressed tight by the force of the current, and at best I would get very wet. To Dan this all looked funny, he was laughing loudly but not for long. Dad you need a hand? No Dan I said, this is fun! Grab your shot gun first, then the detector, now me!

"Thanks Dan, I Think You Saved My Life" We had no time to chit chat but get on with setting camp. A space needed to be cleared for camp, doing this went well we were a team no one had to give instructions or stand around. We were now a team. I think the tent was up, bed roles laid out and Dan had supper on the grill in no time flat. It was morning when we went to sleep. As soon as my head it the pillow, (made of my folded jacket). Didn't hear much from Dan ether, maybe it was the rushing water, or it was of the days ordeal, that put us fast to sleep.

Chapter 14 - Day 13, July 16, 1985

Needless to say this was a lazy morning we had water, cool shade, mosquitoes were not all that bad and of the end of the journey was close at hand. Okay Dan today we head for the possible home site number one. It is ahead maybe 2 to 3 miles; it's one I have picked out to look at from seeing the black-en-white satellite photo. It touches the mountains of the Kuskokwim range. Of the 30,000 acres open for selection, it is the furthest most west: of the settlement area but there is more land to the north close to Wein Lake.

We set our compass and set out in the direction slightly east and north of where we are now. Leaving the hills, we're now stumbling through black spruce and thickets of alders. Most areas that were wet were filled with hummocks for the most part, right below the mountain heading for site number one. After a few hours at this particular time we travelled in and around clusters of alders. The clearings have signs of gopher mounds or better known as ground squirrels or parka squirrels. Daniel was taking point and carried the 12 gauge shotgun. Dad! "Come ahead".

Dan was looking down at fresh pile of bear crap. Fresh huh Dad, there also were freshly dug piles of earth dug up by the squirrels. What are the tracks of Dad? My reply was their grizzly tracks Dan, it has just been here. Not too far away huh Dad? I held my hand close over the pile of crap. I could feel the heat rising from it; I would say about 2 min. ago. GEE! Dan says. Dad! Take the gun you take point for a while. We were definitely in grizzly bear country.

There were a lot of ground squirrels in this area and those grizzly bear were pestering him the death. Dan was following close behind now. I in front with the 12 gauge shotgun loaded for bear and ready. I didn't have quite the heart to tell Dan the bear may come up from behind. But we are traveling tight anyway being in a high state of alert. I was ready to pump a loaded shell into the firing chamber. Then, without any warning whatsoever, as I was turning to go around a up rooted black spruce tree stump when all in one moment I pumped in a live round aimed and realized it was only a massive root system with dirt and moss hanging from the roots. For one split second it appeared to me to be a grizzly bear ready to pounce on me. Than with my right fist I pounded once hard on my heart to restart it. "THUMP"

Sometime later we found ourselves on a small rise, just short of the site number one. Using the rifle scope from a distance, we looked the ground over and the area around it. I was not impressed, no big trees, too low ground. Things just didn't feel right. Besides, this was grizzly bear country. Well scratch that site. We will turn northeast crossing the bottoms making our way to the hill of elevation of 1,405 feet. Site number two near the top side facing us and to the west south west good for a sun set view but not south. Time to rest so set on some well-chosen, hummocks with our packs on. Traveling on we come across a good size pond. On the far side, there was the biggest beaver lodge about 20 feet high and 60 feet across, it must be of prehistoric origin, and I have never seen a beaver house this large. It had two giant beaver standing nearby, sometime I will be back to trap those I thought to myself.

Moving on, we were hot, sweaty, but making good headway. When all of a sudden Dan told me to stop I stopped. Dan said walk forward stop. Okay Dad. You're about 15 feet downwind of me wouldn't you say? Yes, I guess breezes from you to me why? Well Dad, I can still smell you. Okay Dan the next creek we come across we will take a bath. We stunk something awful bad.

Then a short distance later a very big Creek was found, running fast and full. Not deep, but comfortably full. We waded across the creek removed our packs broke out the bars of soap, went back to the center of this 30 foot wide creek. Trees with their limbs hung over us giving shade and a place to hang our clothes once we had washed them on our bodies. Raise from the sun showed through and creek had a strong current. First, we washed the clothes while they were yet on our bodies removing them completed the laundry chores by rinsing them. Our clothes were now hanging on the tree limbs and we continue to bath.

"OOPS!" I heard Dan say. He had dropped his soap, it run down the creek out of sight it was gone. Without a spoken word I handed him another. Dan did not have to be told anything he just knew. Thinking to myself now, I better not lose my soap as I was now washing my underpants. I grasp the bar firmly with all my fingers and thumb wrapped around it. But then my undies got lose and went rapidly on down the creek out of sight. Dan laughed and said. Wonder what bear is eating my bar of soap and wearing your underwear.

Than it was play time while we waited for our cloths to dry it was the perfect place to be, sandy gravel bottom not too cold. Dan climbed up onto the bank and jumped off into a deeper hole but in so doing he bumped my glasses into the deep water. Just as quickly, he went after them. Of course I knew they were gone. Not so Dan popped with his arm first holding my glasses up high. Again Dan a great big smile on his face he went on to say he was really surprised to find them.

Then as Dan was splashing and jumping around. He noticed something. Dad! Watch this! What? I said. Look at my feet when I hit the bottom. The gravel moves, not a lot only the yellow stuff. The sun's rays were coming through parts of the trees and when Dan jumped down onto the gravel floor of the creek for a moment yellow, "color" would dance in the sun light then settle back to the bottom. Our day ended on the shore of that creek. This creek was the most refreshing and rewarding finding both iron pyrite fool's gold and FLOUR GOLD's "COLOR", of any creek on our hike.

Chapter 15 - Day 14, July 17, 1985

Sometime during the night and fast asleep I awoke to the sound of very loud swooshing of air. My head was near the door screen, looked out and there was a raging camp fire. Dan! Wake up! We have a fire on our hands. It was our camp fire that had restarted, it had been burned out but not yet cold out because we were going to be using it come morning. This was a thick muskeg root based camp fire pit and the roots in the wind had re-ignited.

I crawled out still lying on the ground, removed the grill, grabbed the frying pan and beat the fire down. Dan ran out with a kettle to the creek that was within a few feet to the creek making several trips, poured water on the fire pit, while I tore into the root system of smoking roots and wetted the surrounding area saturating everything completely. Thanks' Dan now the camp fire is cold out. Another lesson we both had, never go to bed without putting a camp fire cold out that is unattended. In an hour the fun was over and we went back to sleep but I was now sleeping lighter. "We were still moving on"

Morning came; another day was at hand seemed only a short time ago we prevented a forest fire. After breakfast the fire was again put cold out. We were once again on our way, this time to site choice number two. Not much for moss or tangled underbrush this area had been burned of a long time ago so long ago the trees that had fallen had rotted away, it even looked like a good area for trapping one day and for easy trail making. One last main creek was crossed with no problem. A fair amount of house logs and lumber logs were growing along the banks of this creek. The creek had because of the wetter area had saved the timber from wild fires of the past, plus also there was drainage that meant for good white spruce not the stubby stunted black spruce.

Making our way now to the west base of the last hill with the last creek behind that we would be crossing till after the 3rd choice of land I had marked on the map. Crossing this land heading for the last hill there was a mix of tamarack pine and the spindly stunted black spruces. Tamarack is the only pine that sheds it leaves or what is called needles in the fall, then looking like a dead pine in the winter. Tamarack tree fossils tell us that this breed of tree has been on earth a long time along with the different ferns. Then we are entering a birch forest growing above the base of the hill. These birches were mainly white birch. In Alaska we have, black, white, yellow, paper and alder all of the birch family. Being on a gradual uphill incline of white birch was a joy to see.

This area on the hill I looked over well from top to bottom exploring it thoroughly, because from the high altitude photo, I had marked this as a possible homestead site. The good points it had were it had a good amount of mixed timber of size, no wild fires had been here for over 3 hundred years it was an old clean forest, The trees were not close together a fire could be controlled if done careful it could be cleared of rotting fuels and this forest could stand another 300 years but that was about it in the way of my complete interest. We did near the top walk over a depression of a 60 foot in diameter.

It was very noticeable with few trees of any size on this. Walking over this, it had a hollow sounding sound somewhat like that of a drum a big drum. To me it looked like a closed in sagging sink hole with a root system cover. Most likely it was a melting huge block of ice covered by volcanic ash as this was a common occurrence. Ice caves, sink holes and bear hibernate in them.

Other reasons why I did not find interest in this area was there were no flatter or flat grounds on which to have a lawn or garden, most of all, not enough light other than the cooling sun set, I want a full days sun not just a sun set. No real view except for the west mountain range not the range that was pretty, North West cold winds would make for cold winters, nearest source for water was the creek nearly 2 miles off, a forest of trees would need to be removed just to have a southern view of the sun. Nope it did not take long to decide that this was not the land I wanted. Without further delay we set our compass for the 3rd and final choice on the south face of this hill.

We still had the large photo to refer to for other targets but I had very thoroughly a full year before had narrowed it to these 3 choices. Being near the top of this hill we stayed at this level making our way east on the south face, crossing several narrow ridges and ravines all were running to the south. This south face was heavily forested with a mix of birches, spruces and now the different cotton woods no shortage of fire wood here.

We entered a burn that had come from the north ending here on the south face. The wild fire had been extensive to the north and had well recovered with new young growth but there was many standing fire killed trees, that would make good fire wood for heating a house for years to come as long as it could be harvested before the wood rotted, this use of the burn was in my mind's eye. The after math of a wild fire is not pretty but it is nature's way without man's intervention. This crossing was slow because of the mix of dead and new growth that I have written of before.

"Only you can prevent forest fires"

This burn crossing was no fun and dangerous we had to be very careful. So close yet so far from my 3rd choice too, it was hard to control the urge to plunge onward. The day was getting long that means we could make mistakes we cannot afford, a methodical pace must be maintained to insure our safety. To be diligently deliberate is sometimes a wee bit frustrating when the end of the race or project is near.

Look for a space for the tent Dan. An unreasonable amount of time had passed and still not a place to camp. This camp ground (Pun intended) had no openings in the trees for a tent to be set up. If I had not lost my hand axe it would be a simple matter of chopping down some trees. I had my hunting knife and the machete but the trees were a bit large.

Using those would be time consuming so it seemed easier to find an opening. Then there it was a space big enough for the tent. One problem, a tree right in the center DAN! You need to test fire that shot gun on the base of that tree. That's a big 10-4 Dad! BLAM! We watched the tree fall, pitched tent and called it a day thank you God. Or should I have said guardian Angel?

Chapter 16 - Day 15th July 18, 1985

It was another morning that we were low on water. After breakfast I told Dan to stay in camp while I went on ahead for water marking trail as I went. Marking trail was different this time, the young short trees were easy to snap waist high making a clear a trail for our packs and easy to fallow. To my surprise I was soon out of the burn area and an old forest of very large trees appeared it looked so good in fact I turned around and headed back to get Dan. Boy Dad! That was a quick trip! I broke out of this entangled mess Dan. We will pack up and push on there should be no problem in finding water.

We came to the old forest of big trees bigger than we had seen during the whole trip of the birch family. We had seen many large white spruce but not any large birch, some birch here were all of 3 feet in diameter and healthy. This area was my 3rd choice. Entering this I began to see a view. Lots of sun above the forest canopy, facing true south meant for sun during the shortest days of the year and in December.

I was begging to have those good feelings, large birch, large white spruce, big area for a garden, lawn, green house, a drop away 200 foot drop-off for that picture perfect view, excellent soil with no permafrost and good drainage. Yes, I have to remove some trees but I see the possibilities' the future of what it could be. Ever since we had come into the old growth forest still traveling in a line Dan was with his knife re blazing the birch above my blazing by pealing a one inch wide of the outer bark leaving a black ring of the next layer.

The blazing I did was on both sides slashing to the heart wood making where we came from and the way we were headed, again so we could back track if need be. It was a unique marking system 1 inch black line with a blaze below on both sides.

Traveling east yet on the 3rd choice came up to a ridge of good size running north to south, with a sizable well used animal game trail on it. This trail looked to be a migration caribou trail that was used by all animals. The ridge was a natural for having a trail on it. We went over and on down to the valley in search of water and we found a flowing spring coming out of the gravely ground right at the base of this part of the hill. Filled up on water all this was yet on my choice number 3. Then I really wanted to see more, turned back and fallowed the ridge to the top. Up on top we made our way and explored the layout of the ground under the thick burn and new growth. Mind you all this was of trees but I could see that this could be someday an air strip.

It was like I was dancing on air while we fallowed this trail on back down to where we had first reached the ridge. Made our way to the drop away point on this ridge and peered out over the valley of five lakes nearly 600 feet lower then where we stood, Mt. Roosevelt the mountain we had flown over flying to Lake Minchumina, beyond Roosevelt that there was the Alaska Mountain Range some 77 miles standing majestically was the tallest Mountain in North America was Denali Mountain al 20,320 feet then further some 200 miles south out of sight was Anchorage.

"The land then spoke, choose me"

The day was brightly shining not a cloud when we were standing on the edge looking out over the vast wilderness at, "DENALI MOUNTAIN" It was the last inline of this view directly due south like it was on the edge of Earth. "Dan this is where I will build my log home"

Here Dad? Yes right here on this very spot on which we now stand.

For a long moment I stood looking, my mind was like a news room, computing, compiling, analyzing, then the paper was ready to print as a tingling came rushing over me, even the hair on the back of my neck raised. Dan was looking out over this vast wonderful view. When he said, "Just like a picture Dad." Yup! This will be where the front window will be with a deck. Drive that claim stake in. We had now walked 57 miles. "This is it" Set the compass bearing for that large lake. The one we saw the 20ft lodge on the northwest shore; we will pay them settlers a visit. From there we will hop a flight back to Fairbanks. "Let's go"

On down to the flowing spring some 400 feet distance of where the house would be built, we refilled out canteens, with any luck we will be visiting our new neighbors tonight. The spring led to well-trimmed willow thickets the moose had been eating on like cows would to a grass pasture. Willows were maintained shoulder high with an abundance of moose tracks and trails, like a Garden of Eden. This led us to a small creek, traveling was slow but we were determined to stay on course. Not able to see land marks because of being so low we had to fallow our compass best we could, adjusting accordingly to the countless obstacles.

Then suddenly there was this loud, "THUMP! THUMP! CRASH! SMASH! CRASHING! SOUNDS" WOW! Our first close moose encounter of the whole journey. We must have been walking right towards that Bull Moose otherwise he would have let us walked on by. They are that way lying low and hide motionlessly or in this case RUNINGAWAY. This Bull Moose had a 7 foot rack used it like a dozer plowing a path through the small trees.

See where he went Dan! He went the same way we are headed, he has made trail for us. The guarding Angel again Dad. Bull Winkle knew where to go alright; he dozed on out of the heavy thickets into a more open area, larger trees, moss and along the creek bank. Dan was behind me while I was doing my best to fallow the compass heading. When all of a sudden; Dan firmly shouted with the up most commanding voice; DAD! WALK FAST FOR A 100 FEET STOP AND REST. Without hesitation I did as he ordered me. (We had a rule any orders were acted upon without hesitation) none of this huh? Why? How come? Or buts!

At 100 feet I found a log and sat on it. I looked back at Dan; he was making a wide arch staying well clear of where I just was then came to me and sat next to me. Well? Tell me what I did that for! Dan, explained fallowing behind I seen you stepped on wet newspaper, or so it looked, till I saw bees swarming and from the surrounding ground. Those Bees were looking for you Dad. Soon as I seen them, I had you get clear right quick. Thanks Dan, I owe you another one.

Continuing on we walked along this small creek that lead us to a hillside pond shelter and hidden by overhanging trees. This was a hideaway active beaver pond. They went on about their work paying no attention to us while we watched them. Tree beaver were busily chewing the base of a cotton wood, then like lumber jacks they watched it beginning to fall. Two were on the wrong side and moved out of the way. This tree fell part way then hung up on another tree.

That's when I named them "Larry, Moe and Curly" because that is who they reminded me of, each it looked like was blaming the other for this tree being hung up. Then together they wasted little time arguing but moved on to the smaller tree that was keeping the other up. I tell you there teeth slice chips out of a green tree like lumber jacks swinging an axe. Before the first chip hit the ground a 2nd one was in the air. Two worked on this one as the 3rd looked on like he was the boss. It wasn't long when the 3 of them moved away and both trees were down. They took no time in celebrating or shaking paws but immediately began snipping the limbs off dragging them into the pond.

Shows over Dan we now know where the term, "Busy as a Beaver" comes from. We had not gone far walking through an open area of tall what we call up here bear grass, down in the lower 48 it is called slough grass. I was ahead knocking down the tall grass while Dan moved along a short distance behind. "GEESH I gasped!" All in one motion drawing my bear gun jacked a round in it all in a blink of an eye. I held fire and seen it for what it was, it was a 55 gallon rusty brown barrel. It looked like a brown bear, this was bear grass after all, and this grass did not get its name for nothing. Dad you sure moved that shot gun fast, what the heck is a rusty barrel doing in the middle of nowhere?

The barrel had been fire axed in both ends and the part resting on the bottom had rusted away. Dan this barrel has been here for years, perhaps since World War 2 or later during clean-up of old fuel drum depot at Lake Minchumina that of course is only my guess. I suspect these small tundra ponds in this area were dumping grounds in those times. The air dropped empty fuel drums would sink and rust disappearing for ever more. Mother Nature does the cleansing. The drums were air dropped from a big plane like bombs, but first fire axed on both ends in order for them to sink fast. There most likely more in this area but most would have been dropped in the deeper ponds. It might have been during the winter months when this one was dropped thinking it was a pond, I am sure there are more.

This grassy area was a bit tricky because it was a boggy grass covered matted marsh. Don't fallow close Dan and step easy because we could poke through into water and on into it. Thread lightly we may have to deviate our heading if it gets more dangerous. The grass moved up and down, even the small scrub black stunted trees here and there would sway and bob, it was like we were walking on water with pontoons on. Keep an eye on each other Dan; get that rope out and handy. Aiming for those small trees one by one we moved on from one tree to the next for firmer footing. It was an eerie feeling to see trees move wobbling about.

Remembering this open area that we were now crossing from seeing it where we drove the claim stake, we had only to make our way to the wood line then on a ways further where the lake would be but not being able to see over the trees we could not be sure. The floating span of grass was now behind us, it was a good feeling to be back on solid ground where the trees were no longer wobbling. I get motion sickness easy but during this walk I was more concerned about one of us falling through then to feel sick.

After traveling some distance in this forest, I felt we should have by now arrived at the lake, it was getting late in the afternoon. Not hearing any water fowl was telling me we were far from a lake. Dan! Time to climb a tree! These trees don't have any limbs on to aide me to climb Dad. "OKAY DAN", it's my turn to climb a tree; we need to find that lake.

Took off my pack shinnied up crossing my legs, hugging the tree and went on up this skinny tree. I could see two lakes one hard right and the other hard left of our heading. OKAY DAN! Well which way Dad? That way, set the compass for that direction. Climbed down told Dan we are in between two lakes had we continued on we would have hit the 3rd lake some day tomorrow. We would have missed our intended lake.

How did you do it Dad? Do what? Climb that tree? I told him what to do and he had seen how it was done. I have to try that Dad. Dan had no problem and had now learned how to do something else. It was now 2 A.M. when we reached the lake where we see beaver swimming, ducks, sea gulls, and two cabins. One straight across from us the same one we had seen from the hill several days before and the other was to our right far away that we had not been able to see till now. Only the hard working beaver were awake and one was swimming close by us pulling a tree branch. Dan wanted to shoot the beaver for fresh meat, Dan we would wake the people and this is not the time.

Chapter 17 - Day 16th July 19th 1985

Camp was set up after 2 A. M. this morning, It had been a long day yesterday but today was bright with a slight wind making this one mile wide lake a little choppy close to having white caps. Not like last night when it was smooth as glass. The wind was a blessing in the way of blowing the pesky mosquitoes away.

Pancakes for breakfast, the mix that only needed water, pancakes proved to last us a long time and was filling making for good breakfasts. Looking over this lake it was round, lined with a mix of trees. At the right was the outlet to the south with a small hill of about 40 feet high. Looking northward from the outlet a quarter of a mile was a cabin set back from the shore about 300 feet. Swinging more left nothing was seen in the way of people sign till straight across from us was a right pretty sight.

A cabin on a hill that was about 20 feet above the water line set back about 100 feet. There was nothing else on the lake that I could see for sure there weren't any air-o-planes. According to the list of claims on the map I have, on this lake alone there should be six or more dwelling sites. This was the map I needed, to know where the claims were in order not to over stake on someone's claim if I wanted land down here. Once claimed, whether proved up on or not the land is tied up and was imposable to claim over at the BLM recorder's office. Even if the person that claimed was not returning to complete the proving up requirements to qualify for paten.

Look Dan over near the shore of that cabin that we thought to be a 20ft lodge. What is that Dan? Looks like a yellow raft with two people Dad! I see now there flying a kite. Well I'll be darn! The only place to fly a kite is on the lake. Okay Dan let's get their attention hand me the signal mirror. It had no effect, apparently because they we looking up at the kite they did not notice the flashing light reflection.

Okay Dan time to use the cannon, (shot gun) this will get their attention. Being sure of aiming it at a safe impact area, I fired" BOOM! The gun shot echoed back and forth. All this time Dan continued using the signal mirror. Looks like we have been seen there reeling in the kite Dan said, YES! Now they were headed back to shore, then they went up to the cabin, rather than packing up the tent we waited for a response.

The one came back to the raft and began to paddle towards us. Mind you out on our side the lake it was rough white caps now the lake all of one mile across with a raft was not going to be speedy. The man in his raft was slowly making his way towards us. This was no big raft but a small rubber one. Hope he knows what he is doing, I thought to myself. Then with-in hailing distance I called out. A-HOY IN THE RAFT! Then a reply; you okay! Yes we both said at once.

While he still paddled towards us, introductions took place. His name was "Mark Weronko" he and his 4 year old son Toby were flying a kite. Mark had taken his son back to the cabin grabbed a first aid kit and came to us. Why the first aid kit I asked? I thought you were down in a plane accident. Then Mark asked us how did you get here? We walked in from "Lake Minchumina". Marks immediate reply was; walked! No body walks in, everyone fly's in.

Mark pulled his raft ashore and we shook hands. A long visit ensued; Mark was a talker and was full of questions. He suggested we leave our packs, tent and gear to come back for it tomorrow. This is only a 3 man raft he explained and you know how that is always overrated. I know, pointing to our tent this is rated for 4, we laughed.

This was a 3 man raft and we proved it. It was also a wet trip, a real balancing act, the raft could have had more air and water was lapping all the time in on us as we spread apart best we could.

Mark was a talkative friendly fellow; he talked the whole way across. It was no wonder why Mark was talkative he, his wife Katie and son Toby had been out here for all of 90 days with no one else to talk with. Mark only had the one paddle otherwise I would have helped. Heading into the wind was interesting every time he stopped paddling we drifted back a ways. Nearing the shelter of the lee side we were gaining more headway.

The shore was abrupt no sand bar or weeds just water right to the tree line of leaning black spruce with a small space of a bank. From there on up through the trees was a well-made path. It felt good to step out onto solid ground after that wet bobbing raft trip. Mark led the way up to his cabin and introduced his wife Katie and their 4 year old son Toby. Then told them our names and we had walked in from Lake Minchumina. The words I will never forget as long as I live came from, "Toby Weronko." Upon being told we had walked in said.

"YA KRAZY"

My immediate reply was, "You got that right!" Then we all laughed. If there was any ice it evaporated instantly. Katie was a nice lady made us to home didn't have to talk much Mark was doing that, telling us there whole story. First Mark showed us around his place. The cabin they had been working on was built on top of stilts of wood dug down to hard solid ground. Well vented to keep the perm a frost and cabin from moving or settling. The cabin was in the stage of being worked on but it was closed in and had a roof, window and one door. Porch stringers were there but not yet decked. The length was 16 feet long and 12 feet wide, over 8 feet to a celling with a trap door where items were stored. The roof was half pitch, plywood covered by pieces of cut plywood of 4' X 2' small to be fit into a small plane then hauled out here.

Then something you will never see or hear of again is the type of tin he used on top the roofs plywood in water proofing for hard cover. In the days then, there was in the printing of newspapers what is or was known as printer's plates. Light gauge metal sheets the size of a double page of a regular size newspaper. Somehow the print was on one side and was blank on the other; these plates were use in running off the pages. Use only for the day's newspaper. Then would be normally sent back to be melted back down and run into new rolls for the newspaper companies to be used again.

But somehow Mark took these plate off the hands of the News Paper Company in Fairbanks, named the, "News Miner" for .05 cents each. There as light as paper made of aluminium shiny on the one side. The other side could be read and was darker in color. Mark had with a staple gun shingled his roof with these printers' plates. Was not a thick hard cover but did the job.

Mark was a frugal person did all the shopping finding deals on everything. When he shopped at grocery stores, he asked the managers for the items that would soon be tossed and was given them for at a lessor price. One item was anything in tin cans that was dented or otherwise damaged on the outside. He bought them at half price, in case lots. Some had no labels but he was so used to a can with no label he had a pretty good idea what was inside. Bakery goods that were past the date were was free or in some marginal cases half price. Mark when in town on his own knew the places he could get free meals and cheap overnight places to sleep.

Mark made good money; working for Northwest Airlines in Anchorage Alaska as a tractor driver that towed the big passenger planes in and around the air ports even in and out of hangers a very responsible job. The cabin had no furniture only a camp gasoline pressure pump stove, small one room cast iron air tight wood stove for heat they simply sat on their stacks and stacks of the cases of canned foods. Buckets and wash tubs for washing, No cupboards just a box for their cooking ware. Mind you they we only getting set up and had done well with the time and what they had.

They had done a lot of hard work in building the cabin. The logs had been dragged in by hand that were in the woods nearby but many had been rafted and brought up from there beach head. Mark had no experience in building a log cabin but had been a genius in the way he did the log walls. He would round notch the logs joining at the corners some getting the log close down to the next. Then with the chain saw run the running chain bar saw between the logs lowering them more, in time of several passes and lowering the round notches brought the logs together making for a tight fit teddies' and diligent work of art.

Mark had cut free hand with the chain saw 2" X 8" planks for the rafters. Floor joists were made of flat sided logs. Beneath he had 10" fiberglass insulation with metal ¼" screen to hold and protect the insulation.

Mark informed us that they were waiting for a pilot friend of theirs living if Fairbanks that was overdue in coming out to bring in Katie, Toby for some shopping and medical check-ups. The plane should be dropping in any day now. He went on to tell us, as far as he could tell no one else was out here on any lake right now. There was a bunch that had claimed the first day it was open but most left and never will come back.

Others have not started to prove up but have time too. He said he was not a veteran and had to live in a proven habitable dwelling for 5 months each of 5 years and had not yet been inspected to have a habitable dwelling, only then will they count my time living here. That will be Katie and Toby while I go and come from work. Katie is not too keen on the idea of being out here by herself. So it will be hard to prove up in the time I am allotted.

Chapter 18 - Day 17, July 20, 1985

We slept up stairs last night while Mark, Katie and Toby were slept in the room below. Then after breakfast Mark pumped up the raft full tight of air so I could get everything of our stuff in one trip. Fortunately the lake was as smooth as glass going and coming back was no problem. I was relieved no bear had come by and destroyed anything while it sat there most of the day and all last night, I was always thinking about that. That guardian Angel, Dan was looking after it. Today Mark paddled us to two other places on the lake all had been long abandoned, with each one Mark told us there stories. On our way to the one at the south end we paddled by a bull moose that paid us no attention. Seems he knew Marks yellow raft and was not in the least worried of him. I snapped a few photos here is one.

This cabin we were going to now was the Carries, a young couple. He had intended to stake land far way up the hill about a mile from this shore but after trudging through a tangled mess some distance carrying a pack and a 5 gallon bucket changed his mine half ways there. Came back to the shore and said this will be better. Then they went about building a crude cabin made of small fence post diameter trees living in a tent at first like everyone did. By winter they had moved in. Nothing had been peeled; chinking of everything they had was stuffed between the small wood sticks, from paper, fiberglass, rags but mostly card board tacked to the walls.

This stopped the breezes but not the cold. The small wood heating stove was not by far enough to keep warm. Their intentions were good; they built a cold entry with a door, then a door to the inner room. They had a midsized generator and lots of gasoline. Made a swinging hanging double size bed no mattress other than the moss they dug up. Hundreds of gallons of gasoline were used to keep them warm under their electric blanket while in bed which I expect was a lot of the time. Mark told me more but it would have taken a book to write it all down. In time they gave it up. It was not for the lack of trying, they gave it their all then were flown out. Many dreams are dashed in life there's was one.

The saddest story was back past Marks on to the north end. The Weeks, Father, Mother, Daughter and her boyfriend. There all I saw was permafrost posts holding an octagon sill made from big spruce logs.

This was meant to be a big log home. A few things went deeply wrong here. Number One: They made a deal with a pilot that they were to make an air strip in exchange for flying things out to them. This sounded good and they could work out a guiding fly-in business from that, for moose hunts and the like. They cleared trees filled in the low spots with timber beams, cleared brush it was looking pretty good a lot of their time went into doing this. All this time they lived in a 10 man tent. The pilot never showed back, leaving them high and dry.

Number two: No plane ever came. They run out of food. This was the time period that others were living on this lake and the next lake closest were two cabins being lived in. The father and boyfriend in order to eat were forced to hunt for food. Thinking a plane will come in time. To keep the mosquitoes at bay they had smudge fires making smoke to help keep the blood sucking bugs away. The father killed a bear and it was too much meat to keep in the summer so they held a block party, in this case a two lake party.

Well you guess it the remains attracted more bear, more kills more two lake parties. Still no plane, fall was coming on. The boyfriend then agreed on to make for Wein Lake some 12 miles to the north for help. On Wein there was a lodge and in those days there was no communications except for a ham radio that no one had out here.

The young man made it, taking two days. A plane came back and soon after they left for parts unknown. I heard later one person reported the father shooting bear out of season and was fined. To me it made no senses being victims of a terrible starving circumstance was fined for trying to provide for his family in hard times. Like a game warded told me one time, "you need not worry about me but your neighbor." Back at Marks, we set up tent behind there cabin. One thing that Mark had was a pile of Spam of every kind of spam you can imagine. Katie was good at making it in several different ways. Katie made a good spam sandwich. Or she called them spam burgers, biscuit, slice of spam and a slice of cheese.

Chapter 19   Day 18, July 21, 1985

Last night Mark and Katie told us of Bernard Prudeau on the next lake. Bernard had been there for six months, built a cabin and went back to his home in France. Not being an American Citizen he was not eligible to stake land but wanted the experience so he found a person in Wasilla Alaska that had staked and gave his permission to Bernard to build a cabin. The man that had staked in 1982 upon opening day was one that never came back or had the time to prove up. When Bernard seen his name on the filling map he looked him up asked him if he could build his cabin at no expense using the material on site, then all this man had to do was to live there and finish his prove up whatever his requirements were. But the building time would be done. In any case Bernard only wanted the experience.

The Weronkos' were impressed with Bernard, of his work ethics, his preparedness, skills and his attitude on life. The Weronkos' and the Frenchmen had exchanged visits from time to time by walking even Toby at his early age of 4 walked the whole ways there and back, quite a feat for a little guy. Bernard all of 5 foot tall, was dropped off with his simple hand tools, bed roll, cloths, and several 5 gallon buckets of dry pinto beans by the man who did the staking. A date was set for Bernard to be picked up six months later before the lake froze over at the end of September 1984. April to the end of September was good months to get a lot done.

Mark told us we have to see what he has done, then on my topographic map marked the way to walk to his place. Today Dan and I set out to see this place and got an early start in order to be back in time for Katie's Spam Burgers. On our walk over there we travelled around the lake following close to the shore line as permitted on the moose paths At some point Dan commented, I can't believe that Toby made this walk, he is one tough kid. That he is Dan, like you are; only he is a lot younger.

Toby knows first-hand on walking in this jungle, that's why his first words to us after being told we had walked in from Lake Minchumina were "YA KARZY!" Now on the grassy shore of the lake that Bernard had built a cabin, we found the trail marked as Mark had told us. The trail was about ¼ mile back into the taller timber away from the scrub spruce. This path had been well used by the Frenchmen. Then in a clearing set in the woods was a small gypsy rounded style cabin. It looked like a cabin found in children story books but this one was real. I was already impressed from the first sight. It looked inviting and yet lonely like it had been waiting for company. I said hello "French Mans Cabin", heard a lot about you.

It was built on a low mound of a slight rise, on the ground, it was low in height, flat roof, small in size, a big double pain window at the end we first seen with wood peeled bars to keep the bear from smashing it.

Then on back a small door made of shaved poles tightly fitted with metal hinges for the door to open outward. The handle was of a natural curved wood. Only an outside latch it was a snuggly air tight fit. The door was up off the ground and on a pole flattened floor fitted tight. When opening the door, it was like pulling open a vault door sealed tight no air leaks what so ever. This World Traveller French Man, Bernard Prudeau Using a carpenters draw knife, brace an bit, (Hand drill and drills) cross cut tree falling saw, axe, hammer, rip saw, pocket knife, shovel, small disposable wood stove, cooking kit, made wood pegs (for nails) and a carpenters draw knife foot peddle clamping work bench. With poly sheeting, a window, bunch of printers plates, box of nails and two hinges given him from the Weronkos' built this cabin.

Double walled, first wall was the inner wall peeled, drilled holes for the handmade wood pegs that took place of nails. Floor was peeled, flattened small logs and fitted snug side to side for an even floor. Walls were curved inwardly making it rounded nearing the top. Then the inner walls were covered with poly sheeting. The outer walls then log by log went up with a sheet of poly on the inside of those walls as it went up was filled with earth the spacing was 4 inches, making or sound proofing, dust free and a building easy to heat. The roof was of logs close together in about 2 inch spacing's. Logs were covered with one layer of roofing felt, wrapped with poly sheeting then covered with earth connecting to the earth placed within the walls. Then over that a 2nd sheet of poly sheeting, over that was placed the newspaper printer's sheets. For a hard cover, over that was placed more earth fallowed over with moss.

Note the green roof. This roof (ceiling) had no leaks or condensation but only 5 feet high.

"The French Man for his work, gets an A + grade from me."

Chapter 20 - Our Alaskan Wilderness Adventure Ends

This morning, day 19, July 22 the day after visiting the French Man's cabin, we were served a pancake breakfast. We had given our remaining food to Katie what was left. Then for the next several days we helped Mark on projects that needed to be done and to help offset our extended stay while we waited for the plane that was days overdue. We cut split, stacked fire wood, built a food cache that also served as an observation tower and began digging a root cellar.

When digging the root cellar I found the ridge to be of sandstone, red to black sandstone. Covered by trees and mosses I had not noticed it before but this was a tilted fractured ridge line that went around the lakes shore line.

This made sense as to why the lake was rounded with higher banks on two sides of the lake and in its center at 25 feet deep. This was not a normal shallow tundra pond with grasses but a basin of oil bearing sand stone with very little grass. This so intrigued me I became a tunnel rat and busted sand stone with the tools availed and with fire, with the intent to make a stone cellar unique in nature and self-supporting in structure. I asked Mark what he found while digging those post holes for the cabin. This frozen sand he said. Might be frozen but it will never sink your cabin is on rock.

Photos were taken of the setting sun from Weronkos' cabin, Dan and Mark in front of the cabin along with others that I will cherish for every.

The one of the sun set has been made enlarged and hangs in some homes. One morning I had some sort of an attack. The pain was like no other pain I had before, so bad I had thoughts that I might be dying. This pain started low in my back and steadily became worse. I tried rolling on the ground in the hopes of finding a comfortable position for the pain to go away but nothing worked the pain got worse.

Mark had a medical book, looking up all the symptoms I could barely relate to him while being in excruciating pain. I had the attention of everyone, Dan being very concerned. Mark among other reasons looked for a poisoning asking me if I had eaten any wild water plants there was Hemlock in places along the shore. No! I know not to eat them. The day was a Thursday one of the two days for the mail plane to Lake Minchumina, the only regular air traffic we could expect in this remote area. I told Dan to get the signal red distress flares of ours, to have them ready. The flares are hand held and when fired shoot high into the sky then air burst brightly.

Then we see the plane way far off headed to Lake Minchumina, from our angle being set back from the planes view our area would be general to the back side of the plane. Between the on-going pain and a few words with Mark it was agreed to that he should shoot a flare as the plane was returning back to Fairbanks. The best chance for the pilots to see the flare would be then, plus more would be fired if there was no indication they seen us.

Dan heard it first, it's coming back then it could be seen coming from our right front headed to our left front. It was time. Mark fired a flare; it travelled high then burst floating down slowly in a big ball of sparkling red light. There was an immediate response; the plane rocked side to side the wings reflected in the sun. They see us then flew on being miles away and only wheels it made no sense for the plane to buzz over us. We knew they would report the flare, its location and time to the authorities.

The pain had begun around 9 A.M. then was becoming worse every passing hour. I tried not making a fuss, carrying on or even crying not wanting to exasperate everyone's feelings more. I was cringing enough already but I did not want Dan to leave my side. I held his hand while he tended to my needs and suggestions. I was thinking of words to tell him if the time for me to pass on came.

I passed on supper, crawled into the tent, Dan ate at my side. It was then I got Dan to get me a 5 gallon bucket to sit and try to go to the bath room to relieve myself. It seemed to be helping sitting there; something was passing, what I did not know but it felt well. (A kidney stone?)

During the night I found it better to lay on my one side in a fatal position. Then had Dan with his fingertips lightly touching my skin moving them around over the pain area of my back. It was soothing and the pain left. The time was then 10 P.M... Dan then told Mark I was okay and we all slept well the rest of the night.

Bright and early after breakfast, an orange and white helicopter was noisily hovering overhead circling.

It was the State of Alaska troopers with a megaphone speaker saying something but the noise was to deafening to understand what was being said. Mark rafted out to open water maybe to lead them to an open area on the shore line in which for them to land. The chopper then hovered to shore landed and cut off the engine.

When the blades stopped a Swat Officer in a blue uniform with no cap on his head jumped out with a bullet proof vest and an AR15 rifle held at port arms. He was below us coming up to us, it was then I told Dan do not make a move or touch a gun. Having had experience in the Army knew that no sudden moves should be made at this time. The trooper approached us walking up the hill to us by our tent behind the cabin.

His rifle was held at port arms pointing off to his side and upward with his finger on the trigger guard. The Officer was now a short distance away, he asked is this was a medical emergency? I spoke up telling him it was yesterday but the severe pain I had cleared up last night. He looked straight into our eyes then pulled the bolt on his rifle open and grasps the bullet removing it and removed the magazine as well. I felt at ease at that moment. WOW! You sure come loaded for bear!

The trooper then told us that a lesson was learned a month ago at Manly Alaska. A trooper friend had been shot dead while in a chopper, by a man who went nuts that was killing people at will. We stopped him but we are better alert now. The trooper asked us if there was anything he could do for us now? Mark said yes and handed him a phone number to call the Fairbanks pilot that was overdue. Thank you for coming Officer apparently the flare worked and the mail plane had called it in. The trooper then loaded up, the chopper cranked up and flew off back to Fairbanks. Mark then said when the plane comes he was going to stay, Katie, Toby and us should fit on the plane. Otherwise I would have had requested the pilot make a 2nd trip or contact a different plane for Dan and me.

In the early morning a float plane came right on in without circling cut his engine and drifted to shore. Before the engine had a chance to cool we were in the air off to Fairbanks. I paid for the flight the least I could do. Hour and a half the big City of Fairbanks was just ahead. I then thought wonder if I still knew how to drive. A funny thought I know but thoughts like that happen when not having been behind the wheel for some time. What a sight, cars narrowly missing each other and people milling about. I looked for a float pond but none were in sight, yet we were getting lower to the ground then cars were driving along side of us and then I felt the floats touch water. We had landed on the Chena River in Fairbanks, taxied up to his dock. He then drove us to the storage lot I had the pickup. We had come full circle ending our Wilderness Trek, to now drive back down the Alaskan Canadian Highway to Minnesota.

Next spring 1986, I would be back to work on my homestead in the center of Alaska.

To begin the Adventure of, "Ose Mountain Alaska."

The End for Now.

ABOUT THE AUTHOR

Duane is new to the writing world, but not new to the world of experience. Born and raised In Minnesota overlooking the river valley. Duane graduated Echo High School 1960 he enlisted in the Army 1964 at the age of 21 and spent 3 years touring in Korea as a U.S. Army Engineer.

Duane is married, has 3 children. He started his own company in the Minnesota farming area selling and delivering concrete. Duane was a Scout Master, a survival expert and is skilled at living and thriving under some of the most extreme conditions known to man.

He is also a public speaker, who gives presentations on rural living, homesteading, survival, Alaskan living and interesting topics such as the art of dowsing. Duane moved to Alaska on a whim nearly 30 years ago after surviving shot in the head He and his wife Rena became the last persons to have filed a claim under the Federal Homestead Act of 1862. The Homestead Act of 1862 ended for good October 1986.

Duane found his second wife through the mail order bride system and married Rena of Hamilton Ontario Canada. Rena moved to the Alaskan Homestead to live in a hole in the ground called a Dug Out for 9 years while she and Duane built their 3 story Log Home. They live off the land for the most part, by gardening, solar power and trapping. Rena does the skinning. Duane has so named their heaven on earth "Ose Mountain" and is referred to as Ose Mountain by most.

Duane is now taken to writing and has plans for several books to write living in there log home top of Ose Mountain Alaska. Rena will have a book out on "Wild game cooking and caring of." One thing Duane wrote while living in the dugout one winter day titled River Days Past. A TV interview of Duane and Rena Ose on Ose Mountain completed in 2010 can be viewed one this link. Duane and Rena Ose

Made in the USA
San Bernardino, CA
08 September 2013